Adoption: Philosophy and Experience

Randolph W. Severson

Randolph Severson

House of Tomorrow Productions
4209 McKinney Avenue, Suite 200
Dallas, Texas 75205

ALSO BY RANDOLPH W. SEVERSON

Money and the Soul of the World
Adoption: Charms and Rituals For Healing
Then I Too Will Remember
Can't You Sit Still? Adoption and Attention Deficit Hyperactivity Disorder
A Mighty Time: Talking to Your Adopted Adolescent About Sex
Dear Birthfather
A Letter to Adoptive Parents on Open Adoption

Cover Art: *Lough Gill, County Sligo* by Jack B. Yeats, 1906.
Courtesy of The National Gallery of Ireland, Dublin, Ireland.
Adapted and cover designed by Marilee Vergati.

ISBN: 1-880856-09-3

Table of Contents

The philosopher and the poet are alike in this way:
both seek the marvellous.

–St. Thomas Aquinas

Preface

Robert Duncan once wrote: Our only responsibility is not to lose the ability to respond.

In the chapters collected here, I have tried to be a responsible writer and thinker in a particular field, the field of adoption, by responding intimately, personally, sometimes with angry words, more often with an extravagance of wonder to various issues in adoption.

Throughout these chapters the viewpoint I take is what I would call spiritual. Rather than being a solution to a three-fold problem, I conceive of adoption as the revelation of a mystery. What I mean by mystery here can be captured in the idea, first presented in Betty Jean Lifton's beautiful autobiography, that the adoptee is truly twice born. Born originally from the womb, the flesh, as we all are, the adoptee, through the sometimes unhappy and sometimes felicitous fate of adoption, is reborn into a new reality, a new life, the adoptive family, whose reality is fundamentally spiritual and psychological, that is, born of the heart. As I have often put it, including in these essays, "what is an adoptive family made of if not biology and genes? The only answer can be heart and soul." Further, I believe this transformation is ontological in nature. That is to say, for the adoptee, it penetrates from the soles of the feet to the hairs of the head. Adoption involves and transforms the whole being of all those whom it touches. Whether as birthparent, adoptive parent, or adoptee, once touched by adoption, one is never again the same.

Adoption is a Way, a Path, more akin to a spiritual discipline than an operation of social engineering and adoptive parenting is a spiritual vocation.

And, as with every true Way, one comes to it through fate, through accident, through suffering. As did Dante and Ishmael, all triad members begin their journey by finding themselves Lost in a Dark Wood. Abandoned, alone. All triad members begin their journey through suffering, having been orphaned by their dreams, whether it be, as it is for birthparents, the dream of loving and raising one's own flesh and blood to the joy of maturity, or for the adoptive parents, the dream of having a child of their own who drew life through the union of their own bodies and souls, or for the adoptee who finds him or herself orphaned in fact as well as in metaphor.

The chapters are divided into sections as each seems to play upon a particular theme. In section one, Philosophy, I endeavor to present a cogent and credible philosophical justification for the practice of open adoption, while section II details how that philosophy might bloom first into specific meanings, rituals and practices whose effectiveness is there for all to experience and, second, a poetic revelation of something about the grandeur of the human spirit and the healing power of love. Where the subjects are personal, I have chosen to address them personally, so that the general reader may very well feel as if he or she has stumbled on to something that is meant for someone else. By including them here, I mean not so much as to be heard but as to be overheard engaged in the actual work that I do with individual human beings, triad members whose lives have become interwoven with mine through counseling and therapy. The discomfort that the reader might feel as a result of such unexpected intimacy will be balanced, I hope, with the sense of having learned something in some of the areas of the adoption experience that the general literature has frequently overlooked or having looked, had not very much to say.

The third section takes a look at the adoption rights movement and at the culture of adoption as a whole. The only interest that I would wish to promote is that of the truth of adoption. In the activities and conferences organized by the American Adoption Conference – the subject of one of these chapters – one is more likely to hear the truth than in any other place with which I am familiar. Where the second and third sections in this collection are intensely personal, the fourth is a more strictly intellectual excursion. In the essays included under the title of Social Science/Social Service, I take to task the scientism whose domination of the adoption field I believe to be a disservice to the people we ought to be serving. Though academic in nature, the question of which models are most illuminating and healing of the adoption experience is not academic at all.

Always it is the eternities rather than the "Times" whose lead I follow. Since I am only a writer and a therapist and not a triad member myself, it is only through the generosity and courage of others in sharing the soul of the experience that I have dared to speak at all. To each of them I am grateful and offer this work by way of expression of that gratitude.

PHILOSOPHY

Body Not Bruised To Pleasure Soul:
The Philosophy of Open Adoption

Labour is blossoming or dancing where
The body is not bruised to pleasure soul,. . .

O chestnut-tree, great-rooted blossomer,
Are you the leaf, the blossom or the bole?
O body swayed to music, O brightening glance,
How can we know the dancer from the dance?

W. B. Yeats
"Walking Among School Children"

The poet Robert Graves once defined a "real" writer as anyone who by the genius of words could cause a reader's hair to stand on end. If we use a similar diagnosis for pinpointing the essential issues in the field, then the emergence during the last few decades of open adoption – a bewitchingly guileful term designed to rhetorically outflank opponents – as a standard practice in the adoption field, surely fits the bill. Though not so much among adoption professionals anymore, but certainly among the general public, especially those who adopted under the old system or whose adopted kids have now grown up, at the mere mention of the phrase, hair does often stand on end.

Why? What is open adoption? Why does its employment so bedazzle and provoke? And what philosophical issues metabolize within it? Herewith, a few answers formed first by years of clinical experience working with adoptive families whose adoptive placements were typically closed and also by participation both in the trenches with the families and behind the lines with management in the actual practice of open adoption.

Open Adoption

In its essential meaning, the definition of open adoption is disarmingly simple: it is an adoption form in which communication and contact, talking and touching, between birth and adoptive families, occur both prior and subsequent to their solemn joining together through the adoptive placement of a child. During the planning stages, as well as immediately after placement, talking tends to be at length because there is so much to share in the way of stories, pictures, wishes, hopes, boundaries, expectations; but over time the lines grow quiet as everyone moves on with life, deeper into the business of ordinary living. A picture five years later often finds the birthparents to have assumed a role akin to a distant relative – an Uncle Bob or an Aunt Mary – whose cards and calls are treasured as reminders of the radius of love surrounding the adopted child but who in no way possess the glamour of parental authority. They are relatives who remain relatives instead of becoming absolutes.

Though many claimants that they were first have crowded round of late, open adoption was pioneered in the early seventies by several mid-western adoption agencies. As a coherent form of adoption practice, it drew first breath from the delicate pleas and sometimes indelicate promptings of all triad members – that is, adoptees, birth and adoptive parents – for more information about their past. By the licking of stamps and the knocking on doors, by the tumultuously eloquent witness of dozens upon dozens of autobiographical accounts, and by the courageous creation of a vast underground search railroad aiding those who lost each other through adoption to reunite, all have consistently maintained that heritage – whether birth, genetic, biological, cultural, religious or ethnic – is not like chalk on a chalkboard that can be easily erased. It is not like disappearing ink; instead heritage is scarred indelibly into the soulskin of the heart. In addition, the rise of open adoption owes an element of its exponentially increasing energy to the effort by professionals to solve a riddle over which they long have puzzled, which is the riddle of the extreme overrepresentation of adoptees in the mental health system. Although accounting for only 4 or 5% of the general population, adoptees, especially during the fever years of adolescence, walk through psychiatric unit doors at 4 or 5 times that rate – a figure receiving ample confirmation by multiple, independent sources. Last, and perhaps, in the ultimate analysis, most significantly, open adoption offers professionals the opportunity to break those chains of guilt created by their participation in a system that, whatever be its intrinsic goodness and transcendent merits, was nevertheless built on secrecy and lies. As simple and nonessential as it might be deemed to be by those to whom it is an undeniable given, most adult adoptees in this country continue to be denied the right to know even the place of their birth, much less the names of the man and woman from whose union they drew life. Adoptees are the last minority to be denied by law all their civil rights.

After the first twenty years of open adoption is the story bright or sad? Although two decades is far too short a span of time, a slice of life, to offer any but the most tentative of conclusions; one must say, so far, so good. In a public statement issued in the Spring of 1991, Dan Lang, Director of a Green Bay Agency where open adoption has been practiced since 1974, responded to inquires about the success/failure rate of open adoption: "Since [1974] we have placed a total of 532 infants in adoptive homes through open adoption. The question is often asked: have you had any bad experiences with any of those placements? The answer is **NONE** because of openness."

And to the cautionary word that we ought to wait for additional research before implementing such drastic and decisive change? Another leader in the field, Jim Gritter, has solidly and wisely mused, "Does research prove the beauty of a flower? Do we wait for research before trying to practice the golden rule?" Really, after Husserl and Heidegger, after Jung and Guenon, does anyone really believe in 'hard research' anymore especially in matters touching upon what the poet called 'heart-mysteries?' Do we still not understand that a slide rule and statistics will never catch the human soul?

Closed and Open Adoption

In many adoption agencies, open adoption is superseding the more familiar closed or confidential adoption. In a closed adoption the break is final between birth and adoptive families and thus between birthmother and birthchild. Both social work and legal practice reinforce this break with the object of rendering it complete and irreversible.

Although closed adoption is so familiar to those of us of the present and immediately previous generations that it appears to be the very definition of traditional practice, in fact, to call it such is to betray a historical myopia of the first order. Until the early part of this century, the sealing of adoption records, together with denial of access to those whose fates they traced, were practices of which few had even heard. In 1917, Minnesota was the first state to sanction sealed records, doing so in all likelihood, out of a compassionate desire to protect the mother and child from the potentially soul destroying stigma of illegitimacy. Other states, however, neither jumped on board nor pushed the wagon. Not until the 1940's did closed records and institutionalized secrecy become the rule rather than the exception.

Reuben Pannor and Annette Baran have told us something about adoption in the United States in the 18th and 19th century and what they say is that secrecy in such manners was thought morally reprehensible.

John Boswell, the Harvard historian, has told us about adoption in the ancient and medieval world where the desire of the alumnus, that is, the adopted one, ("the child born of my heart" as one Roman adoptive father put it,) to know the story of his past and to gaze into the eyes of those who gave him birth, was considered absolutely normal. We all know about Oedipus, of course, and Moses. But do you know of Ion as well, the subject of one of the earliest Greek plays, whose entire story is a journey back to meet the woman who gave him life?

The idea, therefore, that open adoption is some kind of dangerous experiment or can of worms is historically inaccurate. In fact, the reverse is true: *Closed records and closed adoption are the experiments. Open records and open adoption are the traditional way.*

Perhaps the question then ought not to be, "Do we have the right to open records and practice open adoption?" Perhaps the real question is: "Did we really ever have the right to close them?"

And the experiment has failed. Closed adoption contributes – in fact, could be said to actually create – within the adopted one what might be called a dual self syndrome, which occurs when a child develops an external, public self, which is the adopted self, which often presents as tough as nails and unconcerned about the past, even as he explodes with anger unexplained, even as he cries with tears that have no explanation; even as he disappears with 'low class' strangers which to him unaccountably possess a hypnotizing magic; or as he scars himself for reasons about which he has no idea nor do others; while below, behind, flow currents, swift, strong currents of the subterranean self, a secret sharer, a spectral self behind the social one, which is the biological, past-history birthself. In closed adoptions these two selves are split apart, one embraced and one effaced, one viewed as real, the other banned as inauthentic, so that the child who was once so full of love never becomes an adult full of life, never full of life because he is unable to find a reality based and socially accepted way to affirm both selves and join them into the seamless fabric of the single personality.

This is not to say, of course, that formation of such a dual self syndrome is the cost of every closed adoption. But the fact that many veterans of the closed adoption system report few problems at least to those who casually ask them, proves nothing. Many beautiful hundred year old buildings still stand in the city by the bay, that is San Francisco. But their existence does not disprove the fact that many buildings have gone down in ruinous smoke and ash in consequence of the terror of any earthquake. And it does not prove that those earthquakes have not happened. And by no means does it prove that there is not a fault line running thought the state of California because the fault line does exist. In a similar fashion, closed adoptions snap a fault line running right down the middle of the adoptee's soul and earthquakes are absolutely certain to occur whether they register or not.

And to the objection that open adoption violates the privacy rights of the adopting couple? Should they not be able to put a lock on their front door and a no trespassing sign in their front yard? Of course, they should be able to lock their front door. . . but it doesn't make much difference if the house is haunted. And that is what a closed adoption does: it turns a home into a haunted house full of ghosts, full of guarded secrets and locked closets, full of questions unanswered and questions that can't be asked.

Why should anyone be forced to live this way – bewitched and haunted by faces at the window, faces seen once, as in a dream, to never appear again?

The Philosophy of Open Adoption

Freud and Jung returned one generation to myth. Campbell and Hillman have led another. In most traditions of depth and psychodynamic psychology, myth sounds as a source of insight into the motions of the soul, that is into the meaning and structure of human personality. And in mythology, many mythic heros, culture bringers, light bestowers, spiritual leaders etc., step forth into the story in the role of an adopted one: Moses, Samuel, Oedipus, Romulus, Remus, King Arthur, the Celtic heroes Cuchulain and Finn, and even down to our own comic book star war heroes, Superman and Luke Skywalker. So what might we deduce from the near universal occurrence of his mytheme? Maybe this: if so many saints and heros are adopted, then perhaps every adoptee has some spiritually high calling, or more humdrumly said, perhaps adoption carries the adoptee into a unique form of spiritual-psychological reality.

After all, what essentially is an adoptive family? What is an adoptive family made of, if not biology and genes. The only answer can be: it is made of heart and soul. It comes alive through a love that has no ground save in the depth of the human spirit. It is held together by a golden net flung out by the Fisher King whose abode is in the heart of every infertile couple. By virtue of his or her adoption, an adopted one becomes a member of a spiritual body formed by love, a family that has its being not in genetic kinship or cellular identity, but in the spirit; and to the precise degree that the adoptive family becomes a *family*, his family, his reality, his identity, his name, the adoptee discovers – discovers in a way that is neither academic nor merely philosophic but constitutes a genuine ontological transformation that penetrates from the hair on his head to the soles of his feet; that soul and spirit are utterly, completely, authoritatively and indisputably real – as real as flesh and blood.

So what is an open adoption? On the first level: a style of forming adoptive families. But on another level, that is, when viewed as Blake said, "not with but through the eye," it crystallizes as an attempt to live on a daily basis, with all the joy and anguish thereby compelled, the essential mystery of incarnation, of how it is that we can be a single person with two natures – spirit, soul, heart, consciousness on the one side, while body, blood, flesh, history, biology, and genetics on the other. If the relationships existing in adoptive families are essentially spiritual ones, born of the frailties and virtues of the heart – an insight corroborated, by the way, by the almost universal occurrence of the adoption metaphor as a way of describing the ideal relationship existing between humanity and the Divine – then an open adoption is the opening of the spirit to the realities of the flesh and history. As Denis de Rougemont has said, "let the spirit come to the aid of the flesh and so recover the support of the flesh and let the flesh submit to the spirit and thus recover peace." Perhaps it would be better if we were wholly disembodied creatures without that "heavy bear that goes with me" as the poet Delmore Schwarz put it, but we're not. Dust, ashes, blood, bone, bile, poor sacks of flesh and bone. And perhaps it would be better if adoptees could be wholly totally and completely twice born. Perhaps it would be better if they could be all spirit. But they can't because they're not; as are not any of us. In an open adoption spirit and flesh can join. It is a mystery. It is a miracle. Body not bruised to pleasure soul.

Conclusion

Advocates of open adoption are sometimes their own worst enemies. For example, representative works often brim with such a wide eyed exuberance and simplified shallow view of human nature as to minimize the pitfalls and the perils that are often associated with the experience. And there are pitfalls and there are perils. Be prepared to cry like a river, I often tell adoptive parents about to take up the path of open adoption, but know also that that river is truly the river of life. Through you, your child and the parents of your child's past may be healed. Open adoption runs over with all the tears and sorrows, the anguish and the pain, that belong to any great drama of the human spirit. Oedipus Rex, one of the first stories of the opening of a closed adoption is many things, but one thing it is not: a happy story. Not all of the animals that stalk the human mind can be as easily domesticated as many would suggest. Whether open or not, adoption will always be painful.

As is life. When asked what happens in an open adoption, Sharon Kaplan Roszia, whose leadership in the field is generally acknowledged, responds with 'Life'. And life does abound with pain, but what binds us through the grim vicissitudes is love, which is what Oedipus discovers after he has acted with such raw excess and suffered through the blinding revelation of his complicity, through pride, in the destruction of his loved ones, when at last he nears completion of his journey. Do you recall the love he finds there, in the end, in the garden?

How Oedipus has passed away no man shall
ever tell—
no man but Theseus.
For in that hour no whitehot thunderbolt
from God came down,
no surge of giant sea to take him.
Some emissary perhaps from heaven came,
or was the adamantine floor of the dead
gently reft for him with love?
The passing of the man was pangless
with no trace of pain no any loud regret;
it was of human exits the most marvelous.

Gently reft with love, then, is how I'd leave you – gently reft with love and rich with knowledge that, as was the way with Oedipus, only the whole truth about adoption, and the whole truth in adoption, will ever set us free.

PRACTICE

To Bless Him Unaware:
The Adopted Child Conceived by Rape

What if it's a child of rape?

As an advocate of open records and open adoption, it is a question I often hear. When the question is raised, winged with emotion, it usually comes from two categories of adoptive parents: those whose motive is to discredit openness by appealing to the worst case scenario – "Oh, the horror, the horror," they say, and of course, they are right; and those adoptive parents whose hearts and souls have already embraced a child whose life leapt into being through a degrading, terrifying act of sexual violation.

To the first group, my response has now become more or less programmatic. I remind them of Coleridge's magical, hypnotic poem about the Ancient Mariner, whose curse and coldness of the heart is lifted when he finally understands that even the most vile and treacherous things, which in this case are the coiling sea snakes, sometimes have their part to play in the mysterious drama of creation. The lines are these:

Beyond the shadow of the ship,
I watched the water-snakes:
They moved in tracks of shining white,

And when they reared, the elfish light
Fell off in hoary flakes.

Within the shadow of the ship
I watched their rich attire:
Blue, glossy green, and velvet black,
They coiled and swam; and every track
Was a flash of golden fire.

O, happy living things! no tongue
Their beauty might declare:
A spring of love gushed from my heart,
And I blessed them unaware:
Sure my kind saint took pity on me,
And I blessed them unaware.

The self-same moment I could pray;
And from my neck so free
The Albatross fell off, and sank
Like lead into the sea. . .

whose rhythmic glow I follow with confession of my own belief that only the truth in adoption can set us free and that even if the truth be terrible about a child's conception it remains the truth, so that only through acknowledgment and acceptance of this fact can an adoptee and his or her family be healed. Only when "a spring of love gushes from our heart / and we bless them unaware."

I say this because I believe it, but over time my desire that others too believe it has dimmed. As I have come to see it, my role is not to convince, but to merely, sincerely share the contours of my own experience. Fear and anxiety about what openness will ultimately mean in adoption is often like a young child's anxiety about the water being cold. There really will be no getting over it until he takes a breath and steels himself and dives. And while the water will be cold at first, a deliverer of icy, cascading chills, the momentary shock will soon seem worth it as the body adapts and the afternoon warms while the cool, blue waters bear up the swimmer into a serene and tranquil bliss.

But for the second group, the parents who sit on the edge of their chairs and hold each other's hand and whose fears are of the known rather than the unknown, I have no easy answer.

To actually have a child, a child of your heart and kindness, who sleeps warm and secure in the blanket after you kiss him goodnight, and to know that this child's life began in horror and that you must tell him and watch his innocence be shattered, and know yourself to be the agent of that shattering, is a duty that no one would wish upon another and that no one who does not bear that duty ought to be too confident about advising others how to do it.

I have no great confidence in what I am about to say. It is only the best I can do. *With such matters we brush against true mystery and ought to tread lightly with our pride gentled by humility.* But it is the advice I have given to couples who have sought my counsel about how to help their child face the fact that the birthfather was a rapist and then how to face that fact and then to accept it themselves.

Since it's always much easier to say what not to do, my first advice is negative. Try not to imply in any way that the explanation for the rape is that *"men are just like that,"* only your birthfather went a little farther than most. Few men are like that. Few men rape. To the great majority of men belonging to every race and culture, rape is an unspeakable crime for which there is no excuse or apology.

Neither, I think, is it wise to convey the idea that somehow our culture bears responsibility for the child's father's act. Undoubtedly, we do dwell in a world where men are encouraged and allowed to think of women as sexual objects existing solely for men's pleasure. In analogous fashion, our world is choked with greed and crude materialism. But neither fact alone justifies nor even explains a *crime*, whether it be rape or the murder of a young man for his Raider jacket or designer tennis shoes.

To offer either of these explanations in an understandable attempt to soften the blow to the child's fragile innocence and self-esteem, as he learns the truth and tries to come to terms with it, is a mistake not only because it lies about the nature of men, but also because it lies about the nature of humanity.

Neither the restlessness of instinct nor the pressures of society explain behavior. To find such an explanation of rape or any other act which involves our entire spirit, one must examine the mystery of human freedom.

So what must a parent do when faced with this task of explaining the birthfather who raped? First, examine your own thoughts and explore your own heart about what *you* believe to be the truth about human nature. In other words, before even thinking of how you will tell your child, you must become for a little while a philosopher. You must ask like Job, "What is man that thou art mindful of him?" Consider why you believe we act? What motivates us? What quickens our desire? What is love? And what part do you believe that sex plays in the cosmic mystery? And do you believe the human spirit is in its essence incorruptible or do you believe that it too can be made intrinsically crooked and warped?

It's easy to dismiss such questions, to brush them away like fuzzy cobwebs. Or to consider them pretentious, suitable for philosopher and preacher but not for you. But whether we accept the role or not, to our children we are all philosophers; all teachers who with our smiles, our tears, our laughter, and most of all our examples are constantly communicating to our children our innermost thoughts, our heartfelt invisible beliefs about the nature of the universe. So at least for an evening, with your spouse, perhaps beside the fire, or later alone by yourself in the quiet of the night, ponder these questions and as you consult your own heart, consult as well the Holy books and beliefs of your own tradition. For me, it is always the Bible to which I return. And the High Romantic poets.

Then, reflect on rape. If you are a man, can you even imagine doing such a thing? Have you ever felt even something like a desire to possess the shapeliness and soul of a woman even against her will? And what have been your thoughts and feelings when hearing jokes or reading the paper or seeing media images that depict scenes of sexual violations? And you might give some thought as well to how *you* might respond to rape, to sexual violation of the intimacies and boundaries of your own body.

And if you are a woman, do the same. Because you are a woman, you are much more likely than a man to suffer such a crime. Therefore, you may find that access to your own feelings comes much quicker but wounded by far more pain and vulnerability. Perhaps, too, if possible, you might want to at least talk to or visit a local rape crisis center to witness personally the trauma, the anguish, the awful horrific shock of rape. To talk to a victim and even to a rapist would also be an experience, or rather, an ordeal, worth suffering through both for the first hand knowledge and for the heart awakening that might thereby occur.

What you may lose through this inner quest for the grail of your own most deeply cherished beliefs is the hope that your child will ever "understand" the reasons for a rape, and especially not for the rape to whose occurrence he owes his life. What you may come to "understand" is that rape is an evil, a terrifying, terrible evil which cannot be understood, since its origin lies not in biological, material, social or psychological factors, but in the mystery and responsibilities of the human heart.

And yet, since we are created in the image of God, as nearly every spiritual tradition teaches, and since we are beings of the spirit, although rape is a sin, an evil, for which there can be no excuse, the rapist himself, the child's father, is also in the depths of his spirit created in the image of God and is by virtue of that fact worthy of love, respect and forgiveness.

So what do you tell an adopted child whose conception occurred because his father raped his mother? You tell him the truth. You tell him the story, and you tell it to him as the story of how he came to be but not necessarily as his story, since he too is a spiritual being with free will and so can choose never to imitate his father in this act. The sins of the father are not visited upon the sons. And he may be told that even as it is only a part of the entirety of his story, so it is only part of the entirety of his father's story. And that to hear all of his father's story is a gift that you hope will come to him.

Further, you can tell him the story of your own reflections, your own wrestling with the demons and the angels. You can tell your child how you first felt when you heard about the rape – the fear, terror, anger, and revulsion – and how you have come to terms with it, the meaning it once had for you and the meaning it has now. And regardless of how you feel now – whether angry or detached, bitter or reconciled – you can tell him how you hope to one day feel, as we all hope to one day feel: *full of love and charity that hates the sin but loves the sinner.*

Should you tell everything? No, no more than you would explain to any child every detail of his or her conception.

And should you use the word rape and when should you use it? With some reservations, I recommend that you not use the word itself until you feel the time is right. My reservations are twofold. I've been a parent long enough to know how hard it is to tell your children the truth about something that will cause them pain, and how easy it is to soften and defer it as long as possible. And I've been both a parent and around adoption long enough to know that when the truth is deeply painful, the right time often never comes. Further, if the right time never comes and your child discovers the truth, the real truth, on his own, you have not only deprived him of your own strength and support in coping with it, but have also added a new truth to his map of reality. This new truth is Mom and Dad cannot be wholly trusted.

When I say "not until the time is right," I mean right according to your heart instinct, the one that says, "go ahead now even though it will be hard." Do not trust the advice of professionals who are called "developmental" psychologists because they can never do more than offer broad generalities about approximate ages and aptitudes for understanding. My experience working with children has taught me that they nearly always know much more than we think.

But though the whole truth and specifically the word "rape," to which even a child will have an "in the gut" reaction, should be deferred until the time is right and you are certain that your son or daughter understands the meaning (which, developmentally, probably occurs sometime in late latency; that is about 10 or 11 years old), a parent should always tell the truth. So as soon as your child asks or becomes aware – and only your love and instinct will hint at its emergence – that it "takes two" to make a baby, he or she should be told that his birthmother and birthfather were not in love and perhaps did not know each other well, and that they did not "make love" but rather "had sex" even though the birthmother didn't want to.

And when there really are two sides to the story, the child should know from the first that his birthfather said that he did not rape your birthmother, or did not believe, for instance in date rape, that he was guilty of rape when he and the child's birthmother had sex.

In addition, the child should know what you believe. And if you don't know what to believe, the child should know that too.

But do not forget the birthmother. It was she who as a result of the act will probably go through the rest of her life afraid of things that go bump in the night, afraid to walk alone, trembling for no reason, crying out in anguish in the night. From all accounts rape is an evil from which it is almost impossible to heal and from which it is impossible to ever recover the innocent completeness that existed before the crime. In your effort to help your child, do not forget that from a certain point of view, it is not the adoptive parents right, nor even the child's right, to ultimately forgive the father. It is the birthmother's right alone. To tell the story of conception in a way that underplays her pain and horror is to do her a terrible injustice.

(Do we still not understand that the failure to do her justice, to honor her as the source of life, curses the love and hope and growth that can sometimes occur through adoption. And do we still not understand that it is not she that curses us, but through our denial we that curse ourselves?)

Though the child of a rapist (which is a fair and accurate thing to call a man who has committed rape, though no single word can ever exhaust the meaning of a man's life or character) can never really "understand," nor can he be expected to, he can perhaps with the help and healing love of his parents, and under ideal circumstances the help and healing love of his birthmother and birthfather as well, forgive the birthfather and find a way to contemplate the mysteries of fate with a kind of wordless, loving, grieving wonder. *To such treasures of spiritual grace a little child can sometimes lead us.*

Where Grief and Joy Divide:
Thoughts Upon a Placement Ceremony

Not so long ago in adoption when a couple received a child into their family, they typically would drive to the agency where everything would be in preparation. The foster family would be there, ready to slip out the backdoor so that the adoptive parents would not see them. In those days, secrecy was all. The secretaries and workers would all flock around, cooing over the bright-eyed innocence of the child, taking turns rocking and holding and cooing. All would be smiles and happiness. The warmth and glow would capture everything. In fact, the sensation that settled into all of us much resembled that of Christmas morning. And then the adoptive couple would appear at the top of the stairs, lay eyes upon the baby, and the joy would take your breath away.

And then the new mother would take the child into her arms.

And then we could all breathe again.

Somewhere far away would be the birthparents. They would not be much in our thoughts. Happiness does not mix so well with pain.

After a few minutes of small talk and congratulations, the new family would leave, bundling up the child and heading for the parking lot. I used to wonder some about what happened then. What did the couple talk about on their way home? What did they feel? What thoughts came to mind? Since so much mysterious and magical, so much heart and history shaking, had just happened in that moment, how could they cope with and carry the emotion? On other great occasions, when so much is at stake and transformations are so complete, it has been the way of humankind to ritually mark it with a toast, a feast, with sacred words and public celebration. But at the moment of an adoptive placement, no such ritual occurred, perhaps because of our collective wish to pretend that nothing had really happened, that being adopted or belonging to an adoptive family was identical with being born and raised by one's own kind, one's own people, one's own 'blood kin' as my grandparents would have said.

Perhaps, then, our failure to mark the moment was a symptom of our denial that adoptive families are different. But whether a symptom or not, I fear it left adoptive parents in the lurch, unable to completely process, integrate, and absorb within the very tissue of their being the emotions attendant upon such a moment.

Apparently, many, many other adoption professionals were thinking the same thing, because during the last few years "placement ceremonies," where the moment is marked with solemnity and eloquence and attention to its spiritual significance have become the rule rather than the exception.

May I share with you both a description of the ceremony as it happens at my agency, together with a reflection inspired by one particular adoptive mother's words, which showed such graciousness of heart and soul and such philosophic understanding that their recounting here perhaps will awaken your own heart and soul into that special luminosity that some have called enlightenment.

*

Ceremonies at the agency are signaled by the chiming of a bell. With perhaps a little too much overt symbolism, but symbolism in which I take a child's delight, a worker walks the halls with a silver triangle that she gently chimes as a summons to gather in the conference room.

Attendance is voluntary. But everyone is invited. And on any given day, the majority attend, secretaries included. We hustle and we hush. We ask, "whose is it?" and other less polite, less politic questions. As you approach the door, the gentle sounds of a recorded harp will greet you, enchanting the air, gentling the soul and preparing the spirit for the magic of what is about to happen.

When you walk into the room, the wonder enters you, the way a beam of light will shine through a church door window. All eyes are on the child. And there are a lot of eyes, eyes bright and shining and glittering and shifting with anticipation, eyes of friends, family, foster family, birthparents, adoptive parents, staff, and often a minister as well. Although our agency is non-sectarian, we invite the adoptive couple to invite their pastor to participate, to pray or to offer a blessing. Some have boomed glory, some have gently blessed. Some recall the ancient traditions. All remind us that though we have all the virtues, we have nothing if we have not love.

At the front of the room the adoptive parents stand, already with the child. These words are read – a welcome and a poet's blessing.

ADOPTIVE PLACEMENT CEREMONY

On this 1st day of November, 1991, Timothy and Elizabeth are receiving Alexander into their family.

We are gathered here today to celebrate this addition to Timothy and Elizabeth's family. This important and joyous occasion has special meaning for many people.

We wish to acknowledge the birthmother, Caitrin, whose love for this baby directed her decision and plan.

We are grateful to the foster parents, John and Michele Jones, and their children, Robert, Michael, Melissa and Joy, who loved and cared for Alexander while he was in their home.

We celebrate with Timothy and Elizabeth, who are assuming the most important role and responsibility of life, that of being parents to a child.

We welcome family members and friends who are here to offer their support to Timothy and Elizabeth, and to share in their happiness of having Alexander join their family.

We at the agency wish your newly expanded family health and happiness. You will share many things as a family; the most important of these is love.

Timothy and Elizabeth we wish you well in your new vocation as parents of Alexander.

Your children are not your children.
They are the sons and daughters of Life's longing for itself.
They come through you but not from you,
And though they are with you, yet they belong not to you.
You may give them your love but not your thoughts,
For they have their own thoughts.
You may house their bodies but not their souls,
For their souls dwell in the house of Tomorrow, which you cannot visit,
Not even in your dreams.
You may strive to be like them, but seek not to make them like you
For life goes not backward nor tarries with yesterday.
You are the bows from which your children as living arrows are sent forth.
The Archer sees the mark upon the path of the infinite, and
He bends you with His might, that His arrows may go swift and far.
Let your bending in the Archer's hand be for gladness;
For even as He loves the arrow that flies,
So He loves also the bow that is stable.

Kahlil Gilbran
The Prophet (New York: Alfred A. Knopf, 1955)

The words are done and the family is born. All are filled with joy.

Or nearly all. Who are not filled with joy, of course, at this moment are the birthparents, whose loss in the sense of eternal loss of the rights and the responsibilities of parenting this child is now complete.

After this moment, the child will truly be twice born, born not only from the bodies of his biological parents but from the spirit of his adoptive parents as well. So, who could expect the birthparents to do anything but cry, with tears streaming down if not their faces then in the quiet places of their hearts?

After the ceremony, everyone really does go his separate way, for the ways really are now *separate*: Workers pass back through the doorways of their office, while adoptive parents now pass through the doorway of their dreams. But birthparents, at this moment, what doorways do they pass through, except that which leads into the veil of tears?

So many times after such ceremonies it is the birthmother whom I watch leave.

Unlike the adoptive parents who are always surrounded by friends and family, the birthmother usually has no one, unless it be the single social worker whose counsel has probably seen her though some tough times indeed. But no one can see another person through a moment such as this.

What happens on her drive home? What dreams turn to ashes? What hopes turn to dust?

It is always the aftermath that makes such ceremonies bitter-sweet. It is seeing the difference at this moment between the adoptive parents who, crowded by joy, walk down the stairs *with others* and the birthmother who walks down the stairs *alone.*

Can anything be done to make that walk less lonely? On the practical level, obviously. Birthparents can be encouraged to bring some friends or family; workers can be sensitized to reach out not only to share in the joy but also to feel the grief and pain as well. And someone can always say something.

Thus the second part of this reflection – for someone did say something once and those words, which were so unrehearsed, so utterly spontaneous, did heal, did, as the poet said, *"in the deserts of the heart/ let the healing fountain start."*

The words came at the end after the official words and actions were all said and done. Holding the child in her arms, the adoptive mother asked the birthmother if they could pray together and then taking the birthmother's hand in her own, putting her own hand over it and then clasping it to the child, she prayed in a voice full of life and joy and wisdom:

> *"Dear Lord, who has blessed my family today with a joy and love that truly is surpassing, bless this woman, too, for though I cannot understand" – and then she gazed deep into this 'other woman's' eyes – "your pain, your grief at having to give away this child, God in his infinite wisdom knows it, shares it, feels it and I hope I can feel it someday too and I know he will heal us both and in healing us heal our child who is not really our child at all but who is His, whom he gives to us because he loves us, as we must learn to love one another."*

Where grief and joy divide only God can join – God in the sense of a love that surpasseth understanding. The rest is silence.

First Steps:
Opening a Closed Adoption

A child's first steps always seem a miracle. There he stands, motionless with wonder: the trembling legs; the swaying balance; the eyes glued on you and then the arms reach out, and then . . . it happens, to praise and clapping; to squeals of joy and laughter.

What a gift it is to be present at such a moment! And what a gift it is to be present when adults reach out, overcoming doubt and fear, to take their own first step into some new adventure, whether the adventure be a literal one – a marriage, a first job, a new career – or something more to do with the reasons of the heart, as when we reach out to share our love and vulnerability.

Today many adoptive parents, whose children came into their hearts and homes through the old closed system, are reaching out to agencies for more information about their child's birthfamily. They're asking if there are letters and pictures available. And they're asking sometimes for a phone number too.

To be present at such a moment, when the letter arrives or when the call comes in truly is a gift for those of us whose lives are committed to the adoption field.

We marvel at the courage and the love it takes, knowing how hard it is to take those first steps into such an unknown world.

Why would a parent take such a step? What would be his motivation? What would she be thinking? In our experience the motivation is always love and what the parent is often thinking is simply "I know this is best for my child. I know it's the right thing to do." How do they know? How do we as professionals know that fostering such reconnection between adoptive family and birthfamily is the right thing to do?

Let me share with you a few stories.

Let me tell you about the telephone ringing one morning and a quiet voice on the other end, asking almost apologetically for the name of the birthfather of her 4-year-old son.

"He just wants to know his name", she said. "And I know it's right for him to have that name. I mean what could be wrong with him just knowing a first name. It would mean so much to him. He might not feel so disconnected from everything if he could just know the name."

Let me tell you about a 16-year-old adolescent who had come in for therapy. Bright, blue eyed, bouncing in and out of her chair and with all the typical adolescent obnoxiousness that makes the typical adolescent so difficult to bear. Adoption wasn't her problem. Being obnoxious was her problem and refusing to go to school or do her chores or follow the rules at all. So I thought, although she insisted that adoption was her problem, all she wanted to know, she claimed, was a little more about her birthmother.

Believing, as I did, that the adoption issue was a red herring, I told her that if she really wanted to know about her birthmother she should sit down and write out 25 questions she wanted answered. My thought was that such a directive would defuse the issue, since I didn't think she would take the time or energy to do something that sounded suspiciously like work.

When she came in the following week, I commenced with:

"Well, do you have the 25 questions?" "No," she said. A long pause. "I have 221."

> *Question 14. Did she have any pets?*
> *Question 15. What was her favorite color?*
> *Question 16. Did she love me?*
> *Question 221. Will I ever see her?*

Let me tell you about the letter that came to the agency from a 10 year old boy.

"Dear Mom and Dad. I'm in the fourth grade. I keep wondering what you look like. Well, I'm sending a picture of me. Send one of you. Please, my name is Samuel. What is your first and last name? They won't let me send mine or I would. Do I have any brothers and sisters? Please write back. Please. Please send everything you know. I want to know you."

With great courage, love and with the simple understanding that roots are real, even if they are only part of the story, the parents of each of these children followed up with the agency and in each case we were able to help. In each of these cases, we tried to enlighten without intruding. In each of these cases, we tried to help by giving hope.

To take these first steps is what adoption professionals refer to as "opening a closed adoption." This is something different from open adoption and it is something different as well from being open with your child about their adoption. Most adoptive families, in fact, have always been open with their children about the fact that they're adopted, but what we haven't always been open about, neither adoptive families nor adoption professionals whose advice the families were merely following, is the child's birth heritage.

What each of these stories illustrates is just how important that heritage can be to the unfolding identity of an adopted child and how both love and life furthering it can be when such information is sought out and shared by two adoptive parents who truly do have only their child's best interest at heart.

What one more story will illustrate is how good and freeing it feels for an adoptive parent to reach out not only to receive, but also to share – to share the joy and happiness of parenting with the birthfamily, whose gift of love and trust made possible that joy and happiness. Here are words of joy written from an adoptive mother to her daughter's birthfamily on the occasion of her daughter's selection for the Homecoming Court. For me, its eloquence is overwhelming, proving the old truth that love is like the sunlight: There's enough for everyone unless we choose to remain standing in the shadows.

Tonight your daughter was royalty. . . tonight she was candidate for Homecoming Queen at her high school. I thought of you and how proud you would have been to see her. I was very proud and happy, and although she wasn't chosen as queen from the final-

ists, she was a beautiful princess, and cheered for loudly by many friends in the school. . . the evening was special with flowers and relatives and picture-taking.

She has been a queen in our house for over 18 years now. . . let me tell you a bit about her.

What followed were three pages of a daughter's life seen through a proud mother's eyes, and then,

So thanks again, from the bottom of my heart, for sacrificing your daughter so that our joy could be made full. I'm sure it wasn't easy for you or her father, but how much you gave to us! As her mother, I have thought of you often – birthdays and special occasions like tonight especially. . . wondering if I could have made the sacrifice you did. She is a queen for whom we are thankful!

Elizabeth's Adoptive Mom

Don't let a letter lie unwritten in your heart. Don't let one from your child's birthfamily lie unread in the file either. Take that first step. Let your courage be the bridge. Call the agency or attorney through which your family came to life. And keep calling and keep calling until they show as much courage as you.

Sibling Reunions

A Letter To Those Who Have Been Contacted

"I have something to tell you," says your mother or father, wearing a downcast look, one that you haven't seen before or at least not seen that often.

"What's wrong?" you think. "Who died?" "Mom, Dad are you all right?" are the words that you find your lips are forming, while your brow wrinkles and a shiver jolts your spine.

You brace for the worst. But what you hear is something like, "Before I met your Dad. . ."

Or, a letter comes: "Dear. . . I don't really know how to begin this. You don't know me but. . ."

Or, the telephone rings. Or, there is a knock at the door.

On the other side of the conversation or on the other side of the door is a stranger who, with a few words or an improbable story that, nonetheless, at once rings true, becomes what you didn't think you had: a brother, a sister, another sibling.

You catch your breath. You freeze. You pause. You mumble awkwardly. And then, your whole world shifts.

Who are you? You are one of the shadow people of the world of adoption, one of a mass of men, women and children, of all ages and races, whose beliefs and backgrounds are as different as night and day, who long ago and far away, in a time and place about which perhaps they knew absolutely nothing, lost a brother or sister to adoption. Through your growing up years and in all likelihood on into the ripeness of your maturity, you have had a brother or sister somewhere whom you didn't know existed.

But now, as a consequence of someone's courage or someone's commitment to finally tell the truth – because, even after all these years, the truth is still worth telling – as a consequence of the courage and love of your mother or father or the courage of a long lost brother or sister to reach out to you, you know. You've been told or contacted.

Through the years the professional adoption community has paid you scant attention. Frankly, the needs of other triad members – the lingo used to describe birthparents, adoptive parents and adoptees – seemed far more pressing. And because we didn't attend, we didn't learn and so offered precious little guidance about the best response to the words, to the call, or to the knock on the door that reveals the "secret"; not a skeleton in the closet but a living, breathing person on your doorstep who is related to you by flesh and blood.

And so much does depend on your response. Rejection, denial, the cold shoulder or the sharp rebuke can be ruinous for you, for your mother or father and for the brother or sister who now you have a chance to know. And without some guidance, the chance for a disastrous mistake is heightened.

But, all that has changed over the last few years thanks to the courageous work of many in the search community and a few pioneering professionals, whose names and books are listed at the end of this book.

What follows is an attempt at guidance based on some of what I have learned through listening over the last few years. I mean to share with you what has been passed on to me by birthparents who have suffered in silence, grieving for the loss of a child through adoption but afraid to tell their other children for fear it would estrange them or would jeopardize the love and trust built up over a lifetime; by adoptees who have risked the kind of rejection from which it is difficult to recover in order to simply affirm themselves as who they are and, therefore, who they have a right to be; and from siblings reunited with their adopted brother or sister, who have opened their hearts and doors.

And yet, this is not a manual or a how-to book. Instead, it is a reflection meant as an invitation to your reflections, insights, and self-discovery. Whatever else reunion is, it is always this: a voyage in self-discovery.

*

Regardless of how the revelation comes, the initial reaction of nearly everyone who learns for the first time of the existence of a sibling about whom they did not know is relief mixed with shock. More often than not, something like this has been suspected for a long time. Whether or not the suspicion ever actually entered consciousness, one often hears after a sibling reunion statements such as: "I always thought. . ." "You know I was just sure that there was something, but I could never put my finger on it." "I remember that time that Dad or Mom said. . . and I didn't understand why they would say such a thing." "You know when I asked why I couldn't have a sister. . ." "Mom always seemed so nervous at the doctor's office." Sometimes dreams and fantasies have entered into the twilight zone, hinting at the existence of a brother or sister who haunts the house despite the fact that no one has ever spoken about him or her.

Things do go bump in the night. And one of the things that bumps the loudest is a family secret.

Relief often comes, as well, with the discovery that it wasn't something worse, especially when contact and even a relationship between the adoptee and the birthparent has preceded the *news*: "I thought he was having an affair." "I thought they were going to get a divorce." "I knew something big had happened. I thought it was bad, but I didn't want to pry." "I wanted to say something, but you don't go poking your nose into Dad's business if you know what's good for you."

So relief then when you found out that you weren't crazy, that yes, something was odd or relief with the discovery that it wasn't nearly as bad as you had feared.

After relief, shock. Wasn't it a shock even if you had suspected it was true? Shock features several well known symptoms: disbelief, denial, immobility, numbness of feeling, and inability to respond. In a sense, shock consists of system shut down: It is a piece of genetic wisdom designed to keep you from acting precipitously in a manner that could cause enduring damage. In other words, shock is a reaction rather than a response.

So don't burden yourself with guilt about how you took the news. Probably you wish you had done or said something different – been more supportive, more understanding, more concerned with the feelings of the person who told you rather than with your own feelings.

If you reacted negatively, if you slammed a door or receiver down, or if you wrote a tacky letter or if you were unable to give the embrace that you knew was needed, or if, at the other extreme, you went overboard with support and welcome to the extent that you left no room for expression of your own ambivalence nor time to resolve it, the blame really isn't yours. It wasn't really "you" speaking, not in the sense of your innermost soul, but rather, you the organism taking over, trying to keep you from capsizing when the winds of emotion were blowing so strong.

There is still time to go back, to start over, to begin again, after apologizing or admitting that you need more time to absorb the meaning of all that has happened. But be certain to say it to the person concerned, so that he or she does not have to agonize through the dark night of fears and nightmares.

Don't make them run to the mailbox or leap at the phone and then be disappointed. Don't leave them to pace and toss and turn and wonder.

As is often the case with adoption, it is not the first thought or reaction that matters; rather, it is the second. It is what you say and how you act after you have had time to come to terms with the reality.

To most of the great questions of life, our first reactions are largely stereotypical, that is, based not upon how we really feel – as if feelings were so easy to determine – but upon instinct (fight or flight) or collectively programmed scripts about things to do and things not to do when confronting a new situation.

But there are few scripts dealing with reunions. And there are no scripts for sibling reunions.

So if someone asks why you first reacted the way you did, respond with "I don't really know" and you will be telling the truth.

*

Anger

After shock subsides, feelings surface. Among them, at least initially, anger often holds first rank. This anger resembles the emotion experienced by many victims when they return after a trip or errand to find that their house has been burglarized, the door kicked down, their intimate belongings rifled through. A man's home is his castle, his private space, his living zone, and no one ought to be able to enter it without his permission. When someone does, he rages righteously at the sense of being violated.

So with our families. They, too, in a certain sense belong to us and we to them. We expect them to have boundaries that are fixed and clear. And no one ought to be able to cross them without our invitation and approval. When someone does barge in, or appear to, we can't help but tense and stiffen. Who is this person? And what gives him the right to come into our lives and make himself at home?

Who is this person? This person is a paradox. He or she is a stranger who is also your kin.

If you are someone who expresses anger easily, who barks and bites, who stomps and yells, this feeling may come as a rush or wave, so that there is no question that you feel wronged. But if you have trouble with anger, as most of us do, since anger, real anger, as in holy wrath or righteous rage, remains repressed, a ticking time bomb in our collective belly, you may feel it only in your belly, or in your neck and shoulders. You may find yourself with a flare up of an old psychosomatic problem, or you may find yourself snapping at and irritable with friends who have done you no wrong. Or perhaps the whole emotional tone of your world may seem to acquire a kind of rear view mirror glare, so that you just can't focus or find any relief. Your soul may pulse with an underground current of hostility.

Some honest self-reflection now can help you admit your anger – how could you not be angry upon discovering that there's been a stranger in your house, so to speak, and that he's evidently been there a long, long time without your knowing it? Self-reflection may also help you to identify the *cause* of this anger.

What is the cause? Who is the cause? Who has wronged you? Tread carefully and honestly with the courage to scrutinize your every thought, because all too often, siblings in a situation such as yours direct all the anger toward the adoptee, as if the whole incredibly complex and emotional situation was somehow the adoptee's fault. Ready and waiting to reinforce such a thought are a multitude of rationalizations where the bottom line inevitably is: "Why wasn't the sleeping dog let lie?" *If only your brother or sister had just kept quiet. . . not been so curious. . . not been so obsessive. . . if only they had just been happy with their own lives and families. . . wasn't there something a little screwy about the need to dig up all this stuff. . . Who is this person? This person is a paradox. He or she is a stranger who is also your kin.*

Before you get too carried away, it would be well to linger for just a moment over just who these thoughts concern: your brother, or your sister – someone who has every right to know who he or she is and from where he or she comes.

Often sibling reunions are aborted by just this internal process. You, or someone like you, decides that it would be better not to meet or make contact, and anger, whether acknowledged or not, provides the necessary emotional fuel to remain firm in your decision. Essentially, it boils down to this: You're angry so you withdraw.

But if you withdraw, what you will be withdrawing to is a lie, pure and simple. Unfortunately, living a lie is not all that hard to do. It is not unlike carrying shrapnel from an old wound. Nobody sees it. Nobody knows it; but over time it may work its way through your system and cut you to the heart.

If you don't withdraw, if you seriously and courageously face and express your anger, what you will likely find is that you are angry not with the brother or sister about whom you've just learned but, instead, with your mom or dad, the parent with whom you share your new found sibling. This person whom all your life you have loved and trusted and who loved and trusted you has let you down. He or she is not the man or woman whom you thought you knew. How could he have done this? How could she have done this and never told me? The pillar of respectability, the hero on a pedestal did something beyond what you could have even imagined – and hidden it away. Kept it secret. You thought every door into that parent's heart was open. Now you find that one was closed.

What may keep you from admitting this is your own fear and trembling about what such a thought would mean. If you can't trust Mom or Dad, whom can you trust? And if you trusted them and they haven't told the truth, doesn't that mean that every truth, every reality, is now suspect? Your whole world may suddenly seem to shatter, every solidity turn false.

So acknowledging your anger and even daring to express it would truly call everything you've known, loved, trusted, and believed into question.

Another darker, more complex situation is the one in which the relationship between parent and child has already been marred with conflict, anger and distrust. In this case, to let yourself feel really angry at your parent for what appears at first to be so complete a betrayal may seem to risk the entire relationship. Better to let it go, you may think, for it may seem like killing her or what she is or was to you.

But here we are back again into denial. This is not a sleeping dog; rather, it is a wolf at the door, and you must respond if you are to be true to the fundamental truth of your life. Your family really is in danger, it can never again be what it was. The question is: *Can it now be more?*

Time may let you see this. "Working through" your anger, as the therapists call it, may allow you to see that what is really called into question is not what kind of man or woman your father or mother is or was, *but what kind of man or woman are you*? Do you have the compassion to accept your parents as human beings with frailties and imperfections and vulnerabilities, with a life filled with mistakes and regrets, but a life filled as well – and you are the living testimony – with loyalty and love? And do you have the courage to let them now be human with you, after all these years of sacrifice, of largely uncomplaining assumption of the thankless, overwhelming and often, grueling task of parenting?

Can you love them for who they are instead of what you need them to be?

Or, what you needed them to have been. If your mother or father is now dead, so that the possibility of resolving the issue directly does not exist, do you have the compassion and courage to do the solitary searching of your heart? This perhaps is the hardest task.

If you do, I think that you will find at the end of this part of the journey that both your heart and your understanding have grown. The rage will quiet, the anger dim, and you'll be ready to go on.

*

First Meetings: Highs and Lows

With insight and the courage to work it through, anger can be resolved. But it will resurface now and then when some event or something someone says touches upon an old wound.

With anger laid to rest, the possibility of a genuine relationship emerges. The relationship may begin the first time you lay eyes on one another. Since, in so many cases, reunited siblings favor one another, the initial meeting may get off to a very slow start as both of you stare and try not to stare. Since it really is unusual to meet a complete stranger who resembles you and may even sit or slouch like you or have a few of what you thought to be your most idiosyncratic mannerisms, the mood of the entire event may seem uncanny.

You may find yourself stared at so intensely, with eyes that look a little wild, that it may be unsettling. Suffer it without saying anything. Suffer it out of some compassion and understanding for your adopted brother or sister. To grow up adopted is to grow up among people who, even if they don't look totally unlike you, nevertheless, will never mirror you in the way of your own flesh and blood. Much of our comfort and satisfaction with our own bodies stems from our physically resembling those whom we love, admire, and trust. To look like your father or grandfather or even your Uncle Harry, whose schnozz would do an eagle proud, is to look like someone who at least at one time in your life probably walked like a king or shone like a mythic hero. On some level, we accept our looks, that is, we form a satisfactory body image, as a result of this identification.

You were allowed to make this identification. Your adopted sibling was not. So his eyes will be embracing you in the way that your eyes and arms once embraced your mother and father, and sister and brother, in an attempt to make the same normal identification. **By those looks and hugs you knew that you were normal. By that look, that stare, he is discovering that he is normal, too.**

Where should you meet? Anywhere you feel comfortable, provided that it is not too exclusively your turf. If you are feeling especially generous, and want to take into account the fact that however shaky you might be feeling, your sibling is probably twice as scared in that it is your family he or she is now becoming part of, you might offer to meet on what to them is familiar ground.

But if you'd rather the space be neutral, make sure that at least one of you has checked it in advance. You will want a quiet, private place to talk where you don't have to be embarrassed to cry because you may very well do a lot of crying.

And, don't bring your spouse or significant other unless you feel you couldn't do it in any other way. Although many siblings talk about bringing their "spouses" so that he or she can "share" in the experience, the reason why he or she usually comes along is for defense, or said more euphemistically, for support. Because this event is going to leave you feeling exposed and naked, best to start that way, with all your defenses left at the door.

So come alone, defenseless, naked as a newborn babe. Remember one of you would have been a newborn babe when you first met had fate been a little kinder. And then in the quiet private place, stare and share and cry.

*

First meetings are the despair of waiters. They tend to go on and on. Souls are bared; guts are spilled; hearts turn inside out. That is, of course, assuming, that you have come prepared to risk something. And to come prepared to risk requires you to have already done some considerable soul searching.

First meetings often end with the feeling of finding and having found a long lost sibling. When they do not, it's usually a sign that some of the underlying issues have not been sufficiently explored. Perhaps the issues are yours. Perhaps they belong to your sibling.

But either way, the dilemma is "What's next?" Ideally, what's next is a little distance and a little time – distance and time enough to "process," that is, to turn everything over a few times in your own mind and to determine the various feeling tones.

A good way to handle this is through letters and telephone calls rather than getting together all the time. It's not at all unusual to want to spend every spare minute together, to want to virtually move in with one another. And no doubt you will both be hungry, especially, the adoptee, to know everything – and everything means everything – every scrap of information, no matter how trivial it might seem to an outsider.

The reason for going slow is that the highs and lows you both will feel are unlikely to coincide. Your emotional life is unlikely to occur on the same timetable. When you are up, he or she will be down and vice versa. In a fashion, the two of you will resemble two new students in a ballroom dancing class where there is no teacher, so that you both must learn together the rhythm of the moves. My advice is to "go slow," otherwise, you'll each step on the other's toes too much. You'll dip when you should have two stepped; bow out when you should have bowed in.

Whatever the pace and tempo that you settle on, the bulk of what passes between you at first will be information. You will be getting to know each other even as you begin to feel something for each other. Knowledge and feeling go hand in hand; indeed, the more they go hand in hand, the better. Although it is not exactly true that we can't feel something towards someone without knowing him, too much feeling without knowledge is usually dangerous. To say, as some might do, that you can't possibly feel anything towards this person, much less the depth of feeling that comes from being brother or sister, is wrong. Some kind of feeling, which is deep rooted, heartfelt and emotionally laden, always corresponds to the "knowledge" that we are of the same father or mother, of the same flesh and blood. Nevertheless, to say that these "kinship feelings" are themselves sufficient grounds for a stable and emotionally satisfactory relationship also is to err. To really and truly love someone, in fact, to even really and truly like them, you have to get to know them really and truly well. Otherwise, what you love is a fantasy, or you love the way that person makes you feel, rather, than the person himself in his own essential individual reality. Either way, it's flawed.

When the natural kinship is felt especially strongly, it sometimes intensifies until becoming almost sexual in nature. The technical name for this is *genetic sexual attraction.* Although the majority of siblings who have discovered one another experience nothing like this, enough do that it warrants mentioning, if for no other reason than to convince the few who do that their feelings are not as abnormal as they might have feared them to be.

Genetic sexual attraction originates in the obvious fact that growing up is a physical experience; which means that growing up together must be a *shared physical experience.* While siblings share their love, they often also share, at least when they are very young, a bedroom and a bathroom and often a bath. In most biological families, the first person of the opposite sex that one sees without clothes on is a brother or a sister. That siblings reunited after adoption would experience an impulse to share in the physical intimacy that is natural and valuable in biological families, but which has been denied to them through their separation by adoption, is hardly surprising. When given the opportunity, who doesn't want to experience something – something intimate and satisfying – that has been withheld from him through no fault of his own?

Should a sibling, however, experience the impulse so obsessively as to want to sexually act it out, the problem may very well arise from a confusion of the physical and sexual. In reunion, as in life, such feelings are sometimes so complex as to be difficult to discriminate. For example, a kiss can be physical without being sexual, as can most expressions of love, care or concern. Further, even when a feeling is overtly sexual – and one doesn't have to be a Freudian to acknowledge that a fleeting sexual fantasy or impulse towards a sibling is not alien to human nature – the decision remains as to whether or not to enact it.

After a reunion, if one does feel sexually attracted towards a sibling, it is wise to seek out counseling with an adoption professional who will understand the feeling and be able to accept it as an occasional feature of the reunion experience; a counselor may also help you to understand the origin of your feelings and the need to analyze them from the point of view of what is best for your heart and soul.

*

Getting to Know Each Other

As the relationship between new found siblings matures, the overpowering, impersonal dimension of the emotions attendant upon reunion typically diminish. What makes the relationship more personal and thus less vulnerable to the influx of impersonal emotions is knowledge.

The more you get to know one another in a vivid and spontaneously natural way, the less your reactions arise from the unconscious depths of your own mind.

Rather than the instinct for sex or power, it is *the will to knowledge* that accounts for the emotional peaks and valleys of most reunion experiences. At first, it is the adoptee's apparently insatiable hunger to know everything, every fact and each detail, with nothing too trivial to omit, that dominates the experience. And you may very well feel dominated by the consuming passion to know everything. After a dinner or a call, you may feel drained and empty, as if someone had somehow reached inside your soul and siphoned off its energy.

It's natural to feel overwhelmed by the adoptee's curiosity. To those to whom the experience is unfamiliar, this need to know may seem obsessive. Comparing it with the level of your own curiosity, you may find your sibling's need to know even more bizarre given that he or she displays such interest in facts that were never very important to you. You may cringe apologetically, with cheeks flushing with embarrassment, at being unable to answer questions that to the adoptee seem so critical, while to you they have never even occurred.

And then you may feel resentful. You may erupt with anger at someone exploiting you as if you were not a person with your own curiosity and fears but a now accessible encyclopedia of information. You may fear that you have been "picked up" so to speak, only in search for information and then discarded when you have fulfilled this role.

What sometimes renders this part of the experience tolerable is the recognition that although the adoptee's curiosity may appear obsessive, in reality, the adoptee's hunger for information about his roots and the shadow life he or she might have lived, is no more obsessive than the concern about freedom felt by the man who lives under a totalitarian regime. The first is a function of the second. Were freedom not denied, it would no more concern him than it concerns most of us who take it as a birthright. So with those of us raised up in biological families: We're not so concerned with the when's and where's and why's of our early years, because it never occurred to us that it could have been otherwise.

So, without expecting so much from yourself that you cannot set a reasonable limit, try to avoid reacting too impatiently to what is unequivocally a legitimate need.

And try to avoid, as well, using the adoptee, and the revelation of the fact of the pregnancy and placement, as a sort of golden key to your own family's history.

After the revelation of any family secret, there is a natural tendency to index every event, every disappointment and difficulty to the secret, as if it were the exclusive explanation. "Oh, that's why. . .," etc. Perhaps and perhaps not. Indeed, probably not. Although the trauma of the placement did affect your parent and probably not a day has gone by without a thought about the child he or she lost, that loss does not explain your relationship. To think that it does is to reduce the flesh and blood, the very human reality of your parent, to a one dimensional caricature. They may not have always known what they were doing, but it wasn't always because of the adoption, or because of unresolved feelings about the adoption. Human beings are simply more complex than that: No single event, no matter how traumatic, so indelibly imprints the psyche as to become forever after the explanation of every deed.

For a time, just as your sibling may use you as a kind of encyclopedia, so in all likelihood, you will be using him, or at least the fact of his existence, which has been for so long concealed, as a key to the riddles of your own and your family's history. Both are stages of the reunion process.

This too will pass. If it does not; that is, if the adoptee's curiosity does not abate, if it really does devour you, so that you feel completely devalued as a person or if you cannot transcend the notion that your parent's and your family's life is really *nothing but* an effect of the adoption, then back off, buckle down and examine your own point of view. Is this really what you want? Is this what you really believe? Is the here and now so unimportant? Is life so one-dimensional?

If the answer is yes, it is because you, not life, have made it so.

*

Family Matters

One of the essential aspects of the reunion experience is its sheer physical joy. What a deep, rich, fulfilling feeling it is to sit on the bed of a hotel room exchanging photographs, or across a table with a bottle of wine, giggling, laughing, telling jokes and stories, or driving around to see the landmarks, the spots of hope and joy where each other's life took shape! There is a special glow, a warmth, an aura that comes from simply keeping company with this long lost being with whom a family soul is shared. And often times, this glow spills outward to incorporate other dimensions of your life, so that immediately after reunion what was drab and dim begins to brighten. Life is fresh and new.

Wordsworth wrote, "My heart leaps up when I behold a rainbow in the sky." Had Wordsworth been an adoptee rejoined to a long lost sibling, he might have written something different, something like, "My heart leaps up when I behold my long lost sister's eyes."

There is thrill and happiness, glow and pleasure, magnificence and joy, in every reunion. Sometimes there is nothing else to do except to enjoy and savor it.

The joy, however, is not devoid of hazards. In a large family, the sudden appearance of an extra sibling can be an event to which it is particularly hard to adjust. Each sibling needs time to make his or her own connection. And if the family is close, individual connections are very hard to make, since what one sibling does will inevitably involve the others. Old jealousies and angers, old splits and rifts, cannot help but flare. The family pot, with all its repressed resentments and rivalries, may suddenly boil over.

In addition, and perhaps, for you, most critically, there is the question of your "other" parent, your mom or dad who either did or didn't know about this "other" child; which means an "other" woman or man in the past.

The best advice here is to give each other time and to refuse to absorb the new found sibling into the circuit of family life or gossip until everyone has had an opportunity to reach out or to rebuff according to his or her own abilities. In biological families, it is not at all unusual for certain pairs of siblings to be closer than others. The relative closeness and trust depends on multiple factors, such as age, shared interests, how many children you have, where you now live, etc. So do not be surprised if something similar happens in your own family as everyone takes time to get to know each other.

If your family is not only large but also very close, counseling may be required to keep the necessary boundaries intact. The one great danger in this context, which can have lifelong damaging consequences for everyone concerned, is whether consciously or unconsciously you use the adoptee to settle old family scores or to change your status in the family. As soon as the revelation is made, everyone will be eyeing each other to monitor reaction.

If you feel estranged from your father, for example, and wish to be closer, and the adoptee is his child, you might be tempted to be more supportive and accepting than what you truly feel in your own heart. To act in such a fashion is exploitative, because it amounts to the use of another innocent and often fragile and vulnerable human being to improve your own position. In some respects, of course, it is impossible to resist this, precisely because family relationships are so complex and many layered. But by keeping in mind how much potential damage you can do, it becomes easier to try to stand for and in your own individual reality as opposed to acting out or trying to change your part in the family play.

Several times I have seen families, parents and children trying to resolve all their old issues by first embracing the adoptee and then withdrawing again, which, from a psychological point of view, simply repeats the original act of casting out a child in order to keep the original family intact.

To be rejected and abandoned twice in one lifetime by your own flesh and blood is probably beyond the capacity of any human soul to bear.

Also, try to be respectful of the fact that while you and your reunited sibling are related by blood, he or she is also related by adoption, ties and transformations completely real, so that every adoptee is "twice born" as Betty Jean Lifton, the most important writer in the field, has said.

Jean Paton, author of The Adopted Break Silence, puts it this way:

I am one,
Who was delivered into adoption.
And it rests on me until I am dust,
It is my name.

In other words, your brother or sister has another family, whose rituals and traditions and love she shares.

So don't forget the normal courtesies of inquiring after another person's family and don't automatically assume that your sibling will be eager to spend the holidays with your family or to visit during vacation. Other obligations may intervene. When an invitation is refused, it may not be a personal rejection; instead, it only reflects the fact that adoptees who have been reunited with their birthfamilies have multiple obligations.

To unintentionally make them choose or to assume that because they have searched they have already chosen and wish to substitute one set of relations, those of flesh and blood, for another, the spiritual and psychological connections that bind them to their adoptive family, will merely add to the adoptee's already heavy burden.

*

Loss and Forgiveness

By staying true to your own heart mysteries, you increase the chances that this relationship may really flourish. This does not mean that the glow continues to brighten. Instead, it will wear off, dimming over time into the normal radiance of having a brother or sister who is also a friend; in fact, he or she can be perhaps more of a friend than a sibling with whom you are raised, since the intimacy of being raised together can sometimes inhibit the formation of boundaries that are necessary for the cultivation of true friendship. Being in some ways only "like" a brother or sister, sometimes makes it easier to be an understanding, non-judgmental friend.

What dims the glow is grief. As you learn about what has been, you will also be imagining what might have been; that is, what could have been and, therefore, what has been missed. With this comes grief that may leave you feeling weary, sad, full of regrets.

This weariness, which combines sadness with acceptance, and which makes one feel somehow *human and individual*, marks the final term of the sibling reunion experience. And at the same time, it signals the beginning of a genuine relationship, one built on individual reality as opposed to a relationship grounded in fantasy or fear or in meeting someone else's needs.

In feeling weary, you may also feel some guilt about having been kept when this other child was abandoned – or placed or given away – or whatever term seems most appropriate, and the words should change as the feelings do. You may feel the desire to make atonement, to say to this shadow child whose soul and spirit has somehow been present in your heart and home through all these years, *"I'm sorry. Though it wasn't my fault, I'm sorry,"* and in saying those words you will be speaking for all of us: birthparents, adoptive parents, social workers, all who share this poor crust of a planet, where social stigma or economic savagery can force a mother or father to give a child away, relying only on the kindness of strangers to save him.

In the world we live in, adoption can often be a blessing. But adoption ought never to be necessary in the world as it could be. And can we not dream things that never were and ask why not? Can we not imagine?"

*

Let me conclude with a story about someone who found himself in a situation not unlike your own, only he was a preacher, a man who had dedicated his life to faith and hope and charity. Like you, he had been contacted by a sister whom he had not known existed. Having been brought up in a very straight-laced home where there was not exactly reluctance to cast the first stone, having become a minister at a very early age, having most of his life behind the church doors – within a very sheltered environment where nearly everyone he dealt with shared his own beliefs, this man was entirely unprepared for the revelation that his mother, whom he adored and idealized, had at an early age conceived a child out of wedlock and given the child away.

Because he was a good man whose faults were mostly sins of omission rather than commission, the revelation of all these things had caused not so much a crisis of faith – never for an instant did he lose his faith in the ultimate truth of the beatitudes and the gospel of love – but a crisis in himself. The revelation produced not doubt of God, but doubt of self and a loss of confidence in institutional religion where the gospel of love seemed to have been buried under other concerns.

When asked what he had learned from the revelation of the existence of this sister and then later his reunion with her – a reunion that, though rocky, advanced in time to a beautiful plateau of love and understanding – he responded this way.

> *All my adult life I've been preaching, Doc, and trying to live by the Lord's words. I've preached, for example, probably a hundred times on Matthew 25:34-40. You know, the place in the Bible where the people asked our Lord, "Lord, when did we see You hungry and feed You, or*

thirsty and give You drink? When did we see You a stranger and take You in, or naked and clothe You? Or when did we see You sick, or in prison and come to You?"

And our Lord says: "Assuredly I say unto you, inasmuch as you did it to one of the least of these my brethren, you did it to Me."

You know, I said it, but I didn't do it. I didn't feed or clothe too many things except my own self-righteousness and pride. And since I didn't do it, I know I didn't believe it. I didn't know how to believe it. I didn't know how to see the face of Christ in people who were sinners and in whom I couldn't help thinking were just getting their just desserts.

But now after meeting my sister, I know a little more about love and brotherhood. I know a little more about what it means to see the face of Christ in everyone. You know, just the other day, I pulled over to give a ride to some bum hitch-hiking. A year ago I never would have done it, not in a million years. But now I realize that man is someone's brother, that he could be my brother, or could have been and that in the eyes of the Lord, he is my brother and that I ought to treat him that way. I'm not a saint, but I'm not stupid either. I've learned that anyone could be my brother or sister, my father's son, my mother's child without my knowing it. So from now on, I'm going to act like everyone is, or at least I'm going to try to. So you ask me what did I learn from meeting Julia and under-

> *standing how it all happened and that there must be a reason for it happening. Well, what I learned is that the best way to live upon this earth is to turn no one, no stranger, away from your door. It may be your brother, it might be your sister. It might even be the Lord.*

True words, heart earned.

Discipline & Adoptive Families

In they come: the mother, slump shouldered, but her back burner on slow sizzle. She's angry, overwhelmed and about to let you know it. The father, roly-poly or executive slim, washed out and wincing at the indignity of it all. He's here because he has to be or his wife would never let him forget it. And the adolescent, King or Queen of this parade, sometimes bouncing, sometimes slouching, but always hypervigilant in these new surroundings, quick to tongue lash, quick to argue with Mom or Dad before the session. "Sit there," she says to long suffering Mom who shrugs and does her bidding (glancing at you with eyes that say "see what I have to put up with.")

A familiar picture, no doubt, if you work with adoptive families. A familiar picture, you might be thinking, if you do any family work at all. True enough. But what makes the adoptive family different is that adoptive parents are more quick than most to let their adolescent run all over them. (They probably let their four year old run all of them as well, but it didn't hurt as much.)

What collapses adoptive parent backbone? Four reasons.

The first is guilt. On some level – whether we call it unconscious or not is irrelevant – most adoptive parents struggle with some guilt about having "stolen" their child from the "true" parents. Their guilt inhibits them, despite its irrationality.

Another reason is fear. Since they know that the child is not their own, they assume that the bond is weak or at least more fragile than it would be in a biological family, so they are reluctant to come down hard for fear of the bond breaking altogether. To dare to discipline is to risk the total loss of the child. (And who would expect them to do that?)

Rationalization also contributes. "Since the child does not really come from us," so they think, "we can't be blamed for his misbehavior. It's in the blood. It's in the genes. He got this from his birthparents. And once it's in the blood, it's in the blood. What do you expect us to do about it?"

The fourth main reason is lack of *presence* caused by feelings bound up with infertility. In a fundamental way, infertility creates a wound, and the existence of this wound, especially if it continues to weep in secret because the wounded never wept out loud, can rob adoptive parents of their full presence, of their body glow, of that natural, unquestioning, unassuming and entirely legitimate air of authority, that comes from instinctively believing that one's own body is up to meeting all the typical demands of life, including the need to occasionally stand up bodily and make your children mind, even if that means applying a little physical "oomph." Even with an angry, obnoxious, blustering, bluffing adolescent, the need to apply that force usually remains unnecessary so long as a parent retains this physical glow which regularly transmits the subtle, singular message, "if worse comes to worse, I can and I will control you."

What all this adds up to – the guilt, the fear, the easy outs, and the lack of physical presence – is Doormat City.

If the family is to function well and get on with the normal business of living, that doormat is going to have to turn into a flag upon which are written the immortal words *"don't tread on me."*

(Need I point out that my remarks are clinical rather than phenomenological, that is to say, I am speaking of symptomatic adoptive families rather than generalizing about the norm. Obviously, most adoptive parents do not lose control of their kids. However, since according to their own eloquent testimony, so many high functioning adoptive parents do struggle with deep-seated, tenacious and recurrent feelings of powerlessness that seem, at least occasionally, to weaken the will to discipline, perhaps these statements do have some general validity. In other words, when an adoptive parent is finding it exceptionally difficult, despite the best of intentions, to put the skids upon a defiant kid, it is to exploration of one of these four "causes" to which they might turn for insight and self transformation.)

The Technique

The essence of this technique is simply to ask for a detailed account of some recent offense – breaking curfew, running away, shoplifting, failing report card, etc. – and then interrupting the parental report in such a way as to work into the therapeutic interruption a concrete, specific list of all the disciplinary measures, both ingenious and blunt, that could be applied. The therapist manages to do this in the form of a leap to a wrong conclusion. And the conclusion is always that the parents have already applied them on their own, having acted with such force, resolve and decisiveness that their response verges on a kind of parental 'nuke' of the behavior.

Consider this exchange following a parental report that their sixteen year-old son stayed out all night, showing up the next day defying and daring them to do anything about it.

Therapist: "So remind me again of what time he was supposed to be home."

Mother: "1 o'clock on weekends. 11 o'clock on weekdays."

Therapist: "That seems kind of generous to me. You must trust him a lot. So tell me what happened. When did you realize he wasn't coming home?"

Mother: "When he didn't show up by 2 o'clock, we knew something was wrong. He'd never been that late before."

Therapist: "So, he'd been late before?"

Father: "That's an understatement."

Therapist: "So what did you do? Watch the clock for five more minutes then called the police and report him as a missing person?" (To the father: "You threw his clothes out on the lawn?")

Father: (Smiling) "No . . . I wouldn't do something like that."

Mother: "No, I didn't even think to call the police."

Therapist: "You're kidding! A lot of parents overreact that way. And you know the police will pick him up. Surely you felt like calling. Maybe reporting that he stole the car so the police would look for him immediately? No, you mean you kept yourself that much in check? Ya'll sure have more self-discipline than I do. God, you must love him a lot. I'm not sure I love any of my kids that much. Sometimes I get so mad I go overboard. So what did you do?"

Mother: "Well, his Dad went to bed and I just waited for him, worrying myself. . ."

Therapist: (interrupting) "Worrying about all the things you're going to do to him when he got home. Ground him, take the phone and lock it in the car trunk? Pull the plug on money? Take the TV out of his room? Fine him $20 for every minute over curfew the way they do pro football players?"

Father: (under his breath) "That doesn't sound like a bad idea."

Mother: "Well, no, I just worried about him."

Therapist: "You mean at a time like that, when it sounds like he's done this dozens of times already, you were more concerned about him than yourself? That's amazing! I can't ever do that. So when he did come home, what did you do, slap him upside the head a couple of times?"

Mother: (both parents laughing) "No, I'd never do that. We don't use physical punishment."

Therapist: (To the adolescent, who appears to have just entered into a state of shock.) "Boy, you're lucky, when my old man had to wait up for me, I really got it." (To the parents) "So, ya'll don't use physical punishment?" (They nod) " Well, I don't think it is a good idea myself, especially not once kids get older. Probably does more harm than good. But I can understand how parents would think about it. Sort of that tough love stuff. . ." (To the adolescent) "So how long are you grounded?"

Adolescent: "I'm not."

Mother: "We thought we'd talk to you first."

Therapist: "I can't believe your parents care about you that much to take so much time mulling over the right thing to do. Most people just fly off the handle. I'd have trouble not grounding you from the car for three months."

Mother: "Then I'd have to take him to school."

Therapist: (To the adolescent) "Got a skateboard?"

This transcript gives a good taste of the technique. Of course, it's application is varied depending on the severity of the actual offense. But whatever the offense, it's applicable.

The only situation where use is not advisable and likely to have negative effects is with overcontrolling parents absolutely desperate to hang on to the kid. Most parents, adoptive or not, are simply not that desperate and can be weaned from the kid by inviting them into contemplation of the new life and all the fresh possibilities that lie right over the hill as soon as the kid leaves home, and a foretaste of the same new life. At the very least, they'll get his bedroom back and quite a few more good nights' sleep.

What is the goal to be obtained by this technique? Though there's the temptation to name it fancily in terms familiar to various schools of therapy, what it really boils down to is an attempt to *strengthen the parents' hand* in dealing with the kids so that they *stop throwing up their hands* so much and giving in.

In a healthy family, the parents need to be in charge and capable of enforcing rules. This technique focuses on the enforcement aspect.

Are you teaching parents to be cops? Precisely. Every well functioning system needs this enforcement aspect. But not just cops – good cops, whose mere appearance upon the scene is usually enough to calm down a crowd because they know that any act of lawlessness will bring swift, immediate and, more or less impersonal response. "Just enforcing the law, nothing personal." When parents refuse to be cops, they usually end up *judges* which in turn converts their kids into lawyers well versed in every kind of evasion and delaying tactic. And good lawyers transform everything into a trial which is exactly what a therapist will find him or herself conducting instead of therapy if he or she is not careful.

Another way of saying this is that the goal of this technique is to restore parents to their common sense and courage.

When successful, the technique achieves it's goal by:
1) Assuming the best about everyone. When dialoguing with the parents, the therapist is not talking down to them. You're not lecturing or hectoring or subordinating them to your "superior knowledge." Instead, the therapist is simply assuming that they already know everything and that if they haven't done this or that, it's not because they haven't thought of it. Rather, the approach assumes they have but rejected it for reasons into which the therapy need not go. And old clinical rule of thumb, for which there is ample empirical evidence, is that if you treat someone "as if" they were competent, full of the right stuff and tough enough, in this case, the chances increase that they will begin to act in this manner.

In my fantasy, I like to think of it as painting one of those old, rich, solemn colored portraits that seem to ennoble every feature of its subject into which the subject can now somehow step, like a ghost into a picture, merging as it were with one's own ideal nature.

2) Educating the parents, coaching and instructing them, giving them concrete, specific, what-to-do's in order to meet almost every conceivable challenge.

To do this effectively, of course, requires that the therapist has thought through all the disciplinary measures that are possible and that he or she has had enough experience with adolescents to be able to predict their usually very predictable actions. And if his "get tough" counsel can be tempered with a little mild humor and bemusement at adolescent antics, that too is helpful.

Especially must he or she be prepared to repel a barrage of 'what ifs' that will emanate from the parent with the most control in the current situation and the biggest void to face should the adolescent begin to appropriately separate and be on about his business.

3) By serving notice to the adolescent of exactly what will happen should his bluff transform into an actual breaking of the rules. It's just this knowledge, spelled and belled out clear and strong, that can curb an impulse or provide an excuse for extracting oneself from an antsy situation. No adolescent worth his salt is going to make it home by curfew as a result of telling his friends: "Gee, I have to go home now because my mom and dad want me to," but he may very well repair to that age old explanation: "I gotta go home or I'm dead."

In a manner of speaking, this technique transforms an adolescent into a sort of visiting diplomat from a hostile country who is allowed to attend military maneuvers with the object of scaring him with the military might of the home country. After he's stood for hours and watched the tanks roll by, he may very well oppose any attempt by his own country to mount an attack because he knows very well that his forces will be defeated. The display of parental might and muscle thus serves the peace.

"No way I'm doing that" is the thought the technique predisposes because the adolescent knows exactly what will happen and doesn't want to pay the price.

4) It blesses the negative feelings we all harbor as parents, the feelings symbolized in myth by the *Terrible Mother* and the *Devouring Father.* It blesses the negative feelings, the brood of night we all carry within us. One of the great barriers to effective discipline is the media myth – the American family as the Cleavers or the Cosbys – where discipline, real discipline, is unnecessary because all problems, no matter how severe, can be solved in a half-hour. More reality based images of the family can be found in Aeschylus or Faulkner. By reading great plays and novels instead of watching TV, parents would realize that whatever feelings they have about their children, regardless of how ostensibly negative those feelings might be, other parents have had them too. *Adoptive parents are especially in need of such consciousness and blessing of the dark side of parenting.*

5) It models tact and savvy. Clients are always taking their cues from the therapist about how to be, about how to live their lives. That therapists have this power is probably to be regretted since the purpose of therapy ought not to be to make therapists of the whole world, the very thought of which is a nightmare. But whether we like it or not, the status the therapist commands by virtue of his or her position and credentials as a publicly acknowledged "wise man or wise woman" casts us in this role. So best that we assume it with some consciousness and fully aware that our style, attitudes and behavior are likely to be copied. Being able to instruct and impart information and, upon occasion, to direct behavior while enabling others to retain their sense of dignity, their choices and, most critically, their pride is a trait supremely worthy of emulation. One name for such a trait is savvy, which combines strength with sensitivity in order to get things done.

6) And all of this is accomplished in an atmosphere of respect that allows everyone, including the adolescent, to *save face.* This need for saving face, we, as therapists, too much overlook. I once

observed an introductory lesson offered by a famous martial arts instructor and a very spiritual man indeed. After he searched out the eyes of each of the novice and very frightened students, he asked, "What is the secret of fighting?... To never win," he said, and then after a long pause: "But you must never lose either. But by beating a man, by putting him in a corner and humiliating him, you merely guarantee a lifelong enemy when you could have found a lifelong friend." This is good advice for the martial arts, for therapy and for life. No one suffers subordination willingly. *Better to caution indirectly than to confront head-on.*

In summary, a word or two about discipline. First, the word itself, because it's not one that therapists normally use; we prefer instead to talk about "structure" and "limits." It seems to me that we don't like to use the word because, as a general rule, we don't know how to do it or to explain to others how to effectively do it. How many families exit therapy full of bromides about "structure," "limit setting" and full of good intentions but fail at home, not because of a failure of will, but out of a failure of knowledge? Coming up against a novel situation about which the therapist said nothing and faced with a resilient, stubborn, cunning kid who knows exactly what he wants and pursues it with all the single minded zeal and remorseless cunning of an unbeatable attorney, parents surrender. And the reason we don't know how to do it is because discipline is neither a value nor a value-loaded term in most therapeutic visions of humanity. "Growth" is our god term and development, we argue, occurs through a natural process of growth rather than through discipline and training. Most of us consider ourselves in the business of removing roadblocks rather than putting up stop signs.

But discipline is vital to a healthy household. In fact, *it's what makes the house hold* in the first place. For lack of discipline, the roof may not cave in but you're certain to find a few holes in the wall. And perhaps a few doors off the hinges. Parents who can't discipline loose their self-respect. They end by feeling sappy, stupid and blame one another usually, while towards the kid they feel resentment. And then to defend against these feelings parents take refuge in constant criticism which in the long run can destroy a young man or woman's pride. *And a young adult without pride is simply another name for an adolescent with a problem.* And kids without discipline – cagey, cunning discipline that meets them where they're at and hits where they hurt when it is necessary-end by losing their self-respect as well. No matter what the thrill, there's always the morning after. Hemingway once said that "I hate to write, but I like to have written." For adolescents, the opposite rings true. Although they may have loved doing it (feeding on the kick and thrill) they eventually hate to have done it because it makes them feel cheap, low, worthless. Like scum or sleaze. And then, to defend against these feelings, they seek out other kicks and thrills.

Failure to discipline amounts to cruelty to children since what could be more cruel than robbing young people of their self-respect. And failure to discipline an adopted child may be an even more pernicious form of cruelty in-as-much as, when it comes to developing self-respect, an adopted child already must cope with so many other factors. By failing to discipline, we take away their souls just as surely as if we had failed to love and cherish them.

THE ADOPTION RIGHTS MOVEMENT

At the AAC

Reflections on the 1992 Annual Meeting of the American Adoption Congress

A mile high, in a silver cylinder, soaring through gray misty clouds from which a gentle snow is falling, I try to pass the time as best I can. This is a late evening dinner flight from Washington to Dallas, but the dinner is over and lights are being clicked off all over the cabin as passengers, young and old, lean back, wrap themselves with blankets and try to sleep. Two hours remain before landing.

My mind begins to drift across the events and feelings of the conference from which I am now returning. It has been the annual meeting of the American Adoption Congress, which convened this year, ironically enough, in Philadelphia, the cradle of American liberty. I say, "ironically," because, adoptees are the last minority in this country to be denied by law their full civil rights. The American Adoption Congress (AAC) is a national organization dedicated to righting that wrong, together with all the other wrongs inherent in conventional institutional adoption practice.

As is always the case with an AAC meeting, I was impressed by the dignity and professionalism of the organization. The registrations, meetings, dinners, speeches, workshops, even the CEU paperwork, which for professionals is always a chore, ran like clockwork, except that I never felt governed by the clock. Indeed, clocktime itself, with all its pressure to conform and to make of life a rushed, mechanical routine afloat on a sea of petty anxieties, seemed to have been replaced by what my grandfather would have called woodtime, a time where everything gets done when it's supposed to be done without a lot of fret or worry.

While the AAC's efficiency impressed me, the emotion present simply carried me away. For those of us who work as professionals in the institution of adoption, the rage and the desperation, the anguish and the pain that is felt and shared by so many who were once and continue to be our clients comes as a shock; so much so that, during a meeting of AAC professional members, I heard one first-time attendee wonder out loud if perhaps professionals ought to have some prior preparation before attending an AAC Conference, since the rage and pain does come as such a shock and is so overwhelming. To that query, one of the professionals responded – rightly it seems to me – that, for her, the shock itself had been a healing experience in that it had been like a slap on the face to wake her up to the horror of her own complacent self-righteousness about the work that she had been doing. *"After my first meeting," she said, "I went home thinking that I wanted out of adoption. But then I realized that I had never really been in it before. So I decided to get in it, for real this time, and work for change."*

For a professional, part of the shock of attending an AAC Conference comes from the fact that there, right before your eyes, occurs the transformation of the platitude "Adoption is a lifelong process," which smugly slides from mouth to mouth at adoption professional meetings, into a personal story and living flesh that stands to tell that story, and to make stunning, stirring witness.

If adoption is a lifelong process, it is also a soul-deep trauma, "a cumulative trauma," as Betty Jean Lifton has put it, or as Nancy Verrier has called it, "a primal wound."

> *And perhaps to call it merely "lifelong" process belies the truth inasmuch as the subtle spiritual and psychological effects reverberate throughout the generations.*

This thought, as Wordsworth said, "may truly be too deep for tears." But it need not be too deep for thinking. Sadly, our business – and I am more and more inclined to call it a business, for it seems to be the only way to underscore the fact that, however much in this or that individual's circumstance an adoption may appear to be a blessing, money does change hands – has refused to think it, or to think it in a significant enough way as to genuinely transform our practice.

So long as agencies continue to report numbers of placements instead of clients served; so long as agencies are evaluated as a success or failure by funding organizations according to their number of placements; so long as the law defines adoption as the extraction of a child from one family and his placement with another; so long as society as a whole colludes with its taxes and its tears with the idea of adoption as a happy solution to a problem, nothing will have changed fundamentally.

*

Men are gathering," said Robert Bly in his famous Bill Moyer's interview. Perhaps for the first time ever men *did* gather at this year's AAC where we came together for a panel whose agenda was ostensibly to discuss the unique psychology of the male adoptee. This was to be done, of course, from the conventional psychodynamic framework – and with a few gratuitous insults to men thrown in – but like salt that's lost its savor, this agenda and this framework were rapidly discarded as men, both from the panel and from the audience, took the floor to express their feelings – feelings that were often raw, angry, bitter, exposed – feelings that can no longer be ignored.

Following the workshop, men continued to gather in groups of two and three to distill their sense that something unique had just occurred and to discuss how this new energy with its unmistakable masculine intensity might be nourished and maintained.

If a primal wound exists in the adoption experience, a primal wound exists as well in the adoption field. It suppurates and burns. It is the gender rift, the separation of the sexes in the adoption field, which over time has become not so much separation as *segregation,* that is, the exclusion of the male by the female.

With its origin perhaps in the institutionally enforced separation of the birth mother from the birth father (which continues today although the means of separation are far more subtle than in the past) this rift has been reinforced and widened by such a mass of habitual feelings and standard practices as to now seem to be simply the norm rather than a painful, pointless aberration, a cause of cumulative trauma in every male who tries to come to terms with his own experience within the context of the present day adoption system.

In other words, what emerged into the consciousness of many men who participated in the workshop was this insight:

> *It is not men who are in denial about adoption; rather, it is adoption that is in denial about men.*

As one older male adoptee – a man who lived just down the street from the hotel and had more or less wandered into the discussion – shared with me after the workshop in response to my telling him how much I admired his courage for speaking up, "I'm tired of having women tell me how I feel."

By responding in such numbers with such clarity and vigor, the men who attended the Male Adoptee workshop confirmed my sense that all males, whether triad members or professionals, have suffered an injustice at the hands of the adoption professional community which at times has been aided unwittingly and unintentionally by female triad members.

The crystallization of this notion in my own mind arose out of last year's AAC. As is the way so often with a personal illumination, these reflections started over wine, over dinner, while engaged in good conversation with expressive, good spirited friends. In this case, the topic was the annual meeting of the American Adoption Congress, from which many of those who gathered round the table had just returned. One workshop in particular came in for more than, its fair share of criticism. The workshop in question was called "Why Men Don't Search," which from a psychodymanic-psychoanalytic perspective attempted to address the reasons why men traditionally have shied away from searching. The rationale for heaping such abuse on so conventional a workshop – conventional in the sense that the idea that men don't search for reasons related to the nature of the male psyche has become something of a convention in our field – arose from the open records experience in New Zealand, where men have availed themselves of information with the same frequency as have women. When they're given the opportunity, men show themselves to be just as curious and just as eager as women to find out about their past and their birthparents and to pursue relationships with them – this seemed to be the consensus of our company.

What I did not volunteer on this particular evening was the fact that the person who had conceived of the workshop and who had intended to conduct it with great eloquence and insight, drawing as the brochure said, "On myth, poetry and the wisdom of the ages," was me. A personal situation had prevented me from attending the conference, so some other therapist had good naturedly agreed to fill in at the last moment.

(I hasten to add that it wasn't the workshop itself that took it on the chin; it was the idea of having such a workshop in the first place.)

I didn't "fess up" for two reasons: the first of which was understandably enough, I think, embarrassment. I wasn't especially eager to announce myself as the fool in question. But another reason exists as well: I was astonished. I simply couldn't believe that the facts were the facts. I couldn't believe that the number of New Zealand men seeking out their records could in any way keep pace with the number of New Zealand women.

But the facts were the facts and I could not deny them, since among those there assembled was Ms. Mary Iwanek, the distinguished New Zealand sociologist and researcher, whose area of expertise this was. And her point was clear:

> *With all things being equal – a state of fairness which New Zealand, almost alone among Western countries, has managed to achieve – men and women show identical interest in reunion with their roots.*

So, with my shock and my embarrassment, I went home to puzzle out what seemed to me an absolute enigma, inasmuch as the New Zealand experience contradicted what I had taken to be axiomatic: That there are essential psychodynamic elements existing within the male psyche that make it more difficult for the male adoptee than for the female adoptee to confront and come to terms with all of the issues attendant upon their adopted status.

If these psychodymanic elements did not exist or at least did not provide sufficient explanation for why men don't search – for why the majority of adopted men simply will not admit much interest in the subject or much sympathy for the idea that being adopted is being different at all – then what is the explanation for the fact, that at least in this country, whether we talk about agencies, support groups or search groups, adoption is a woman's world and, barring some seismic change, promises to remain so.

So why, then, is adoption a woman's world? Why is it that the workers are women, the clients are women, the searchers are women, the activists and writers are women? Well, perhaps it's because adoption is a woman's world. Perhaps it's because the workers are women, the clients are women, the searchers are women, the activists and writers are women, often strong, charismatic, articulate, committed women who like things done their way; which since they are women, turns out, not surprisingly, to be the woman's way. And the woman's way has become the woman's sway.

> *In other words, what I'm suggesting is that the relative absence of men from the adoption world stems from a sociological fact rather than a psychological necessity, and the sociological fact is that adoption is thoroughly, decisively and indisputably a woman's world.*

To say then that men suppress their feelings, or have more difficulty admitting their vulnerability, or are in the grip of Oedipus, or are in denial about their inner child or their feelings of abandonment, or need the approval of the law, the inner King or any of the other cliches regularly served up in the adoption literature, is a little like saying that, because men, as a rule, don't like baby showers, that the event of birth just doesn't mean very much to them. To spend five seconds with a brand new father, flush cheeked and glitter eyed, with a broad smile and bursting chest, is enough to discredit that particular proposition. No, birth does mean a lot to men, but a baby shower, which is a ritual created by women, for women, where women feel comfortable and in which many women take pleasure, that's a different cup of tea.

So, too, do the issues of adoption mean a lot to men, it's just hard for them to feel comfortable exploring these issues or to find the masculine rites and rituals that are necessary for exploration in a world where there are so few men who are annealed in the experience and thus have the strength of soul and depth of understanding to lead and sanction those rites and rituals.

My point in this chapter is not to explore the genesis of adoption as a woman's world. There are many, many reasons (some rooted in the biological facts of pregnancy) which in an entirely unfair and oppressive manner have historically been treated as a woman's fault, responsibility, and sometimes a lifelong cross to bear should she release the child into what until very recently was not the light but the void and darkness of a closed adoption; some are rooted in the historical fact that social work developed largely as a woman's profession, indeed, one of the few real professions (again until very recently) open to a gifted woman or a woman who simply wanted a decent career; others are rooted in causes far more politically, socially, and historically complex. I would even accept the idea that the genesis of adoption as a woman's world is rooted in the historical suppression of women by men. Perhaps the poets Robert Graves and Gary Snyder are right in their belief that it all got started when the prophets laid ax to the cedar scented groves of the goddess.

I am not denying the fact that the top jobs in many agencies, as well as the controlling interest on the boards governing those agencies, have often belonged to men and continue to be so. I have no doubt that if we really scrutinized *a la* Foucault, the "microphysics of power" in adoption, it would turn out to be a male controlled society.

But what I do want to maintain is a very simple phenomenological fact. What I do want to maintain is that the reasons most men, whether triad members or professionals, stay out of the adoption world, as much as they can is not out of some illusory flaw of the male psyche that makes it more disposed to denial, but because men do not feel comfortable, welcome or understood by an institution which appears at first glance (which is all that many people will give to it) to have become in too many respects almost monolithicly female.

Once I realized just how much adoption has become a woman's world, I got mad – no, I got furious.

But now my anger has matured into concern – concern about birth fathers who do not forget but have been historically forgotten; concern about male adoptees who shy away from the very important search and support groups because of the rage against men they occasionally sense there; concern about the male adoption professionals who leave direct service for the private practice of psychotherapy, as have most of my friends, or in order to begin the long climb of the administrative ladder because to remain on the level of direct service feels somehow to be "unmanly."

And because of my identity as a child and family counselor working mostly with adoptive families, I am most especially concerned about adoptive fathers who seem to lack the fire in the belly that allows a man to stand firm both in his convictions and in his love even at the cost of rebellion by his son or of rejection by his daughter. Because adoptive fathers often fear the bond between themselves and their children to be weak in that it's not being biological, they need this fire more than most if in their parenting they are to proceed as the old Latin motto has it "gently but firmly." Of course, not all biological fathers have this fire, and of course, not all adoptive fathers lack it; but when adoptive fathers do lack it, I can't help but wonder if in some way it's due to their assimilation into an adoption culture and a social work philosophy that has done very little to stoke that fire and much to extinguish it when it began to glow.

Let me again be clear. I am sure that if men were ever to obviously control adoption, the situation would worsen overnight. My observation is that those agencies that are run by women are on the whole much better agencies, both in terms of administration and genuine sensitivity to client needs.

But still, in adoption we face a problem. It has become too much a woman's world with the result that male members of the triad are suffering. And the institutional framework of adoption has become such that this female domination has become self perpetuating. It will simply continue intact and in place until something is done. At this point, having no solution, I suppose I am still part of the problem. But to simply mark it as a problem is perhaps the first small step.

So what is to be done? How can the rift be healed? The workshop was certainly a major step by simply uniting men and encouraging them to express their feelings. In the community at large, further healing might occur if we simply acknowledge the fact that men and women are different and that men, perhaps, typically express their feelings in a way much different than women who tend to be most comfortable and most transformed by expressing their emotions verbally. *For men, it is action by which we express our most heartfelt emotions, the ones for which we have to dig down deep and then struggle to acknowledge.* By our fruits, you shall know us and our fruits tend to be actions, gestures, deeds, rather than mere words, which to us often seem just that, mere words that accomplish nothing. For the male psyche, as Goethe said, "In the beginning was the Deed."

As an example of a delicate, nuanced *wordless* expression of feeling by action rather than words, consider the following description of emotions exchanged between a father and son on the day that they discover that the boy has not long to live:

> *"Come in, please," said the doctor, opening the door for him and his parents to come in. Before the doctor was never there before they got there. They always had to wait on him. "I'm afraid*

the news isn't so good this morning," he said in a voice that seemed to come from a long way off. "The cancer is spreading. There's a number of things we're still going to try and we'll try to make everything as comfortable as possible. There's no reason to give up hope. But it is serious."

Marcus's mother gripped her hands and began to cry.

The rest of the day went by rather quickly for Marcus. He did as he would normally do, spending the afternoon and early evening watching TV, with his parents watching it with him a little bit, but getting up and going into the other room to do things, but then coming back. They all ate dinner in front of the TV that night, watching an old rerun of Saturday Night Live. It was the the one with Mr. Rambo's Neighborhood. It felt good to laugh a little.

After dinner, Marcus went in to take a bath, staying in the water a long, long time, studying his body, the frailness of it, the bruises on his arms from the constant blood tests and injections. His legs looked so skinny to him. He could feel his ribs. After the bath, he splashed on some of his father's cologne, then went on back to bed after kissing his mother and dad goodnight.

He lay there in the dark for a long, long while, watching on his door the pale silver glow and flickering shadows of his parents' TV. After the

> *news, he heard the TV go off and the house fell dark and very silent, with the only light being that from the bathroom in the hall. Then that, too, was blocked out for a second as he felt someone in the room. It was Marcus's father who stood at the foot of the bed looking at Marcus. Neither stirred for a moment, then he felt his father go around to the other side of the bed, pull back the cover and slide in. In a little while, they both fell asleep.*

Would words add anything to this father's gesture of supreme abiding love?

When in therapy a male and female partner understand that both words and actions can be supremely beautiful vehicles for the expression of feelings, healing sometimes happens as the man and woman begin to learn each other's feeling languages and how to translate, so that when faced with a troubling, indecipherable content of emotion, the male will ask himself, *"What was she trying to do when she said that? What was she trying to show me?"* While the female wonders, *"By doing that, what was he trying to say?"* And then as each begins to understand as well that neither words nor actions alone are ever sufficient, the man begins to talk more and the woman finds means other than purely verbal to show the way she feels.

Perhaps something analogous could happen in adoption. We might hear less and less of *"Well, he did come once (for the appointment, to the meeting, to sign the documents, etc.) but he didn't say anything,"* and more of, *"By coming once he said everything."* Concretely, in terms of practice, we might learn that often the best way to integrate a man into a group or process is by *giving him something to do.* During the workshop, one female search group leader whose group has an unusually high male-to-female ratio, reported that this had been precisely her response all along. By putting males to work, by giving them something to do as soon as they arrived, this singularly wise woman had blessed and welcomed their male souls and hearts into the process.

In addition, male virtues such as loyalty and protectiveness must be affirmed as genuine virtues rather than incurring continuous smirks or dismissals as regressive or evidence of denial. Males might find it easier to connect to their birth histories and birth families if the whole question of search could be reconceived and rearticulated in terms of a traditional masculine language that honors the search as a courageous quest, whereby one extends the boundaries of one's heart by giving loyalty and love and sheltering protection to those from whom one originally drew life.

Around ritual, too, we might constellate our efforts, since ritual with its splendor of gesture and its sublimely, glowing incandescences of language attracts and accommodates male energies in a magnificent way. Here, Sharon Kaplan Rozsia's pioneering efforts in work with rituals map a particularly promising path.

*

Ambling through the bookroom, with its colors, fresh ink smell, and geometrical displays, one is struck by how much has already been done in the adoption field, and with how much the AAC has already accomplished. Books, books everywhere, and many by leading figures in the movement. There are the extraordinary books and pamphlets produced by CUB with Janie Fenton at the table; Sandy Musser stands at a wonderful display where I first encountered a poem by Mary Anne Cohen; Pat Sanders is there with her wealth of search material and reflections; John Ryan and Joe Soll also manned tables.

And yet, that this abundance, indeed apparent excess of material, exists is not without its disadvantages. So familiar has adoption become – with all its core themes and related issues – that it has become easy to forget just how unfamiliar and unnatural a reality it is. And, so familiar has it become, that it is easy to deceive ourselves into thinking that we understand it or even understand very much about it at all. And it is easy to delude ourselves into believing that not much more remains to be done.

But much more remains to be done. In many respects only the surface of adoption has been touched. So many souls are suffering. So many are living quiet lives of desperation. And we don't know how to help them.

How much remains untouched and unthought is driven home to me a few days after arriving back in Dallas. After listening to a tape I did on sibling reunions, a birth mother calls to ask if I might have some words of wisdom for her son who has searched and found his long, lost sibling only to be rejected. Fumbling over my words, I have to admit that I have never really thought about it. Once again, I feel like the stupid brother in the fairy tale who, despite all his best efforts, never gets it right. And the fact that it is her *son*, a young man who has suffered the rejection, makes me feel even more silly and ashamed for here is another male, another man, suffering in silence. I invite her son to call me, which he probably won't do, and promise to send on what material I can find that might be relevant.

Later I talk the situation over with my colleague, Carol Demuth, whose insights so often outpace my own.

The young man, about 22, she suggests, was perhaps trying to redeem his mother and to prove himself to her by accomplishing with his quest what she could not.

That her intuition has attained to truth at once seemed clear. But what to do about it is not so clear, and with my masculine desire to *do something* that will help, I write the following letter:

Dear ___________:

Just a few thoughts while I still have your situation fresh in my mind. I move gingerly since we do not know one another and I don't mean to be presumptuous.

I accept your sense, your instinct, since mothers usually do know best or sense best when it comes to their children, both daughters AND sons, though we as males don't like to admit it.

You say you think the disastrous disappointment of being rejected has impaired your son's self-esteem. His branches have been bent as it were so that his manhood has not yet come into full flower.

My guess is that he undertook the search not so much for himself, in the sense that he was desperate to know this long lost sister, but that he undertook the search as a kind of "quest" or knightly ordeal in your service. He hoped perhaps to succeed where you could not, to go into the dark country of the past, of hurt and damaged hearts, and to return victorious, having snatched the treasure, the pearl of great price, from the jaws of defeat. That is to say, he hoped to be the agent by which you and your family were healed. He hoped to do this by bringing all the family together again, the true family that had been lost as a result of the cruelty and foolishness of a world where a mother can feel forced to give a child away.

But he returns from the past, from the wasteland of what might have been but wasn't, defeated. He, too, was beaten, rejected, and cannot heal and so cannot be healed as he, too, belongs to this family, is part of the story.

This may be sounding all too grand and mythical, etc., but in my experience it seems to be the terms in a feeling language, a language that would make them able to share their feelings and vulnerabilities with women, their mothers, daughters, wives and lovers.

So how can you help your wounded healer, your defeated knight? To do too much, I think, is the greatest error here. Talking about it to him will feel like rubbing salt in the wound.

I suggest this. Write him a letter in which you share not so much your feelings but your gratitude. Tell him you honor his courage in all these matters, the courage to be there with you through all these years and to allow you to give so much of your time and energy to others. Thank him for his patience, his understanding; thank him for being the man of honor and decency he is. Then I suggest, if it is not too impractical, plant a tree for him, in his honor, as a way of honoring his strength and courage. Do not ask him if he wants you to do this. Just do it and let him know that it is done and why. As it grows and flowers through the years, so too, I hope will he.

There are other dynamics as well at work which are worth remembering. It might be well to remind him that it was not so much he that was rejected, since his sister hardly knows him, but a past that was rejected to which his sister has not yet come to terms. These are standard kinds of search reassurances so that I'm sure you are as familiar with them as I am.

I'm sending along a few things that perhaps will help by illumining the whole landscape, as it were, of some of the issues. A little booklet, which will be published in the spring, a beautiful poem by Mary Anne Cohen, which touched on some of her feelings about "neglecting" the children she kept and raised and loved and parented in her quest for the son she lost. Also a copy of "Origins," to which I urge everyone to subscribe. There was also another workshop at AAC on male adoptees, moderated by Dirck Brown, which touched on many male-female issues in adoption. To my mind it is worth the price.

My best wishes and prayers for you and your son.

Cordially,

Whether this did help or not, I have no idea since the letter went off only yesterday. But this young man's pain and the failure of our field's extensive literature to address it or to offer any significant help might serve as a forceful reminder of just how far we as a community still have to go.

For this young man, had he walked beside me through the bookstore, there would have been books, books everywhere but not a drop to drink, not a drop of the healing elixir that might restore his soul to equilibrium.

*

Even as the plane on which these reflections commenced eventually touched down, so too must these reflections. Life and work goes on. But even as routine returns to claim me, I find myself looking up from my desk again and again throughout these recent days, remembering a moment's conversation, as we both rushed to catch our planes, between myself and another professional, who described her sense that by coming to this conference she had awakened as if from a dream, a pure fantasy, about what adoption is and isn't. *"A significant part of that fantasy,"* she said, *"has been the language. Never again am I going to use 'positive adoption' language. I'm going to start speaking the truth even if it gets me fired."*

So, in conclusion, I want to confess my own collusion with this fantasy, particularly with regard to birthparents whose decision to place a child I had once called "essentially noble." After spending four days in Philadelphia at this year's AAC Conference, listening and learning from those who work and write and think about adoption, not because they want to but because they must or else, as Mary Anne Cohen has said, "go crazy," nobility is not a word I would use to describe any aspect of adoption. Necessary, yes, sometimes, but never noble. But what in my mind's eye I do perceive as noble and often beautiful, as compassionate and courageous, as wise and glory-wrapped, is the response that many of those touched and tormented by adoption have made to the enigma of their fate:

Sad woman sighing
a mourning tune
shawl all around
hollow eyes, tree arms
black wet sea-salt

memory. . . her lost sons
beckon on the waves
she endures
a stark rock
voice of caves.

–Mary Anne Cohen "Irish Music"

The Primal Wound?

"It is submitted that the evidence is now such that it leaves no doubt regarding the general proposition—that the prolonged deprivation of the young child of maternal care may have grave and far-reaching effects on his character and so on the whole of his future life."

—John Bowlby, 1951

"It is concluded that some of the workers who first drew attention to the dangers of maternal deprivation resulting from separation have tended on occasion to overstate their case. In particular, statements implying that children who experience institutionalization and similar forms of severe privation and deprivation in early life commonly develop psychopathic or affectionless characters are incorrect."

—John Bowlby, 1956

Aware that neither personal testimony nor statistics would finally be decisive, the adoption reform movement has been for two decades in search of a theory around which it might rally and in terms of which it might convince the skeptical or the antagonistic that adoption, that is, the transfer of parenting rights and responsibilities from natal or birth parents to adoptive parents, is traumatic for the child and something to be embraced only as a last resort.

Now let me say immediately that I completely and wholeheartedly support the adoption reform movement and the notion that separation of child from natal parents is a fundamental loss of continuing emotional, spiritual and psychological significance to adoptees throughout their lives. Further, because of this, adoptions should occur only when all other options that would allow a child to be raised by his or her natal parents have been explored and exhausted.

But what I don't support is the theory that now appears to be serving as a rallying point, which is the idea of the *primal wound* developed by Nancy Verrier and clearly and comprehensively articulated in her new book of the same name.

My grounds of dispute are fourfold and may be summed up as follows. I regard the theory as (1) psychologically naive, (2) historically unversed, (3) sexist, (4) operationally destructive. Let me explain.

1. The theory is psychologically naive because Ms. Verrier does not appear to be aware of the fact that her idea draws it resonance and *self-evident* nature by virtue of the fact that it expresses an *archetypal* idea or image. She is in the grip of the Mother-Child archetype, the Pieta, the Madonna with the babe suckling at her breast. By archetypal, I mean that it is a universal recurring image, occurring cross culturally, with great emotional appeal. Whenever it is evoked persuasively and with some relevance to any specific phenomena, it will *seem* overwhelmingly true. In addition, not only will it seem

true, it will seem, when absorbed in it to the point of identification, to explain everything.

A philosophic example might be the Apollo-Dionysus idea, which Nietzsche employed to give an account of Greek culture. When one reads Nietzsche, the idea does seem self-evidently true and to recur everywhere, as if every ancient Greek did nothing in his or her life but eat, sleep and drink this conflict. This is, of course, absurd, as countless classicists have shown, for Greek culture was by no means so one dimensional.

Sexuality, power and religion are also archetypal ideas so that it is possible to develop an entire theory around them which will seem to explain everything, that is, when one experiences reality through this archetype. Other names for the theories reflecting each one of these universal images are Freudian, Adlerian and Jungian psychology.

To take another example, more close to home: Adoption itself is an archetypal idea so that when one is in the grip of the notion it too will seem to be everpresent, the "explanation" of everything. Every popular song, for example, will seem to be about adoption, or, at least, "could be." The fact is that most popular lyrics are about love and loss which makes them applicable, though usually distantly, to adoption, but again while in the grip of the archetype one will feel "certain" that the singer or writer is a closet birthparent or adoptee.

That a theory is archetypal in nature in no way discredits it. But the psychological and philosophical task is to consciously integrate it, which is not synonymous with "rationalization," so that we remain sensitive to other ideas, other images, other values which may have an equal relevance to the experience we are imagining and investigating.

In the emotional sphere, identification with an archetype produces inflation, a torrent and tumult of powerful feelings that carry one away. In the intellectual sphere, identification with an archetype causes one not so much to lose one's wits as to lose one's wit. A sense of humor, a perspective that both delights in and anticipates the unexpected, typically indicates a flexible well integrated point of view.

Another consequence of identification is the splitting off of negative affects and emotions, so that one particular image becomes the very definition of a reality when the fact is that reality is always ambiguous and usually ambivalent. In the case of the parent-child, mother-child relationship, to ignore its' darker, less ideal aspects condemns every mother to instant self-alienation the first time she feels anything but perfect love for her child coupled with the desire to mirror and hold.

2. The primal wound theory is historically uniformed at least about the historical genesis and context of John Bowlby's work, which is its conceptual precursor, on attachment, bonding and loss.

The source of most bonding and attachment theory is twentieth century post war London. In his classic book, <u>Dubious Maternal Affection</u>, J. H. van den Berg, the eminent Dutch philosopher and phenomenological psychologist, thoroughly critiqued the research on which the theories are based. Even if we accept the idea of scientific research as somehow decisive in the human, interpersonal world of the human spirit and soul, bonding and attachment are based on poor science.

Further, relevant is the socio-political context in which the research was carried out.

Following the end of World War II, hundreds of thousands of British and American soldiers returned home to find a more or less high functioning, heavily industrialized society whose need for them was very limited because, in place of all the men who had gone marching off to war, women had moved into the work force in large numbers. In order to find employment for all these returning veterans, it was necessary that women vacate the work force, returning both the employment opportunities and, perhaps, more significantly, the power to men. What better way to psychologically coerce women into "staying home" than to promote a theory that infants and children who were separated for long periods from maternal care would suffer irreparable damage. What better way to convince women that they ought to stay home than to make them feel guilty about "abandoning" their children. And once safely enconsconced back home, their job could be filled by a male.

Bowlby, Spitz and others provided the necessary research and theory. This is not to suggest that any "conspiracy" was involved or that the researchers were doing anything other than the best research they could. It is, however, to suggest, that research and theory always occurs within a specific socio-economic political context whose influence, although subtle, is profound and unavoidable.

In this context of noting that bonding and attachment theory was originally associated with a loss of socio-economic power for women, it might also be relevant to note that the logic of Ms. Verrier's theory inescapably condemns birthparents, for after all, if the worst thing that can happen to a person in his or her life, so that this event creates a "primal wound" in the psyche, is to be placed for adoption, and if this decision is made by a man and woman who regardless of societal pressure and oppression, *could have done otherwise*, then every birthparent who placed a child is personally responsible for this primal wound, for this terrible trauma, although society is also culpable. To load birthparents with this kind of guilt is absurd; it is also ironic for an adoptive mother to be making this kind of charge under the guise of defending adoptees and birthparents. What it amounts to is an adoptive mother saying to her adopted child, "Isn't it terrible what your birthmother did to you?" This is nothing more than a sophisticated version of "Gee, how could anyone give away a child that beautiful?"

3. Verrier's theory is sexist. To the point of absurdity, it underestimates the paternal role in child raising. Two long quotes from Sluckin, Herbert and Sluckin's Maternal Bonding (Basil Blackwell Publisher Limited, 1983) are relevant. "It has been claimed that the maternal deprivation concept served to legitimize the social arrangement whereby mothers are expected to provide the predominant care for their offspring. Is maternal bonding in this tradition? One would be hard put to find reference to *paternal* bonding. The father, in Western society, appears consistently in a role subsidiary to that of the mother–child relationship in the unfolding drama of the child's development. Very little time and energy have been expended in discovering the psychological and sociological ramifications of fatherhood. We saw earlier his relationship with his child referred to rather dismissively as a 'secondary relationship.'

"Richman and Goldthorp contrast such views with the dominance of the social stereotype of motherhood as being natural and 'the font of the emotional support'. *Such ideologies* (and they enjoy a long history) *have, in their view, transformed pregnancy and birth into a female monopoly.* They observe that developmental psychology has a close relationship with social policy and that it provides ideological reinforcement for the stereotype of motherhood. The father tends to be presented as being peripheral; he is accorded the status of genitor and external economic provider supporting the early mother–child bonding.

"The relationship between ideas and social structure is a highly complex, speculative and polemical subject; it is not our task to explore it in detail here. However, it is as well to be aware of the way in which conventional theories of child-rearing appear to assume, or imply, that the contemporary nuclear family with its clear sex role divisions, and ascribed tasks, its emphasis on privacy and somewhat intense emotional attachments, is natural, unchangeable and functional for members of the family and society alike. These assumptions cannot be taken for granted. Paradoxically these same theories are pervaded by a preoccupation with the family's inadequacy and the mother's vulnerability when it comes to performing their 'natural' functions.

"And it is precisely here that the male–female dichotomy is thought to have disadvantageous sexist connotations. When men are portrayed as economic providers, operating mainly outside the home to sustain the family unit, and mothers are presented as the providers of emotional support *within* the home, it is inevitable (if unjust) that mothers are most likely to be inculpated when the children develop problems. This sexist bias is buttressed intellectually by psychiatric theories and child-rearing philosophies."

"We have repeatedly talked about maternal attachment as well as parental attachment, implying that adult-to-infant bonding is not unique to the mother. We have indicated that attachment is a matter of degree and that its strength depends on many factors, one of them being the degree of exposure of the adult to the infant, or familiarity of the adult with the infant. We may now be more explicit and suggest that father-to-infant attachment is not so different in kind from maternal attachment. Certainly paternal behavior soon after the birth of a baby very often resembles in many details maternal behaviour. Paternal attachment, however, often (but not invariably) appears to be less strong than maternal attachment. There are some good reasons for this.

"In the first place, general responsiveness of the human male to infants tends to be less marked. It would not altogether surprise us if there were genetic factors responsible for this. In many, but not all, species of primates males are less nurturing to the young than females, although males tend to be protective both towards the females and their young. Undoubtedly, however, the role of the human male in relation to the young is enormously influenced by culture, custom and convention. Until relatively recent times in Western and Central Europe men were not expected to perform certain domestic duties, including feeding of young infants, changing nappies, etc. The situation in this regard is at present changing rapidly. *It may be that without the cultural overlay men's feelings and responses towards babies would not be all that different from women's.* If, for whatever reason, the responsiveness of males to babies is on the whole less strong than that of females, then specific paternal attachments would be initially somewhat handicapped in their development. In the end they would not perhaps reach the intensity of maternal attachments.

"Secondly in the usual Western family the extent of contact between father and baby is less than that between mother and baby. This may be regrettable, but it is a fact that cannot be overlooked. In the circumstances, paternal attachments have less opportunity to grow at the same rate as maternal attachments; exposure learning, classical conditioning, operant learning, imitation and the rest have less time to operate. No wonder that paternal attachments often seem less emotional than maternal attachments and dominate men's lives less than they do women's lives. What perhaps is surprising is that, despite everything, the attachments of fathers to their offspring are, for the most part, so extremely strong. To say, however, that paternal attachment is essentially of the same kind as maternal attachment does not imply that the father's role in our society is basically no different from that of the mothers."

As is clear from these quotations, to minimize the paternal attachment is also a limitation upon the freedom and power of women. One could even say that it represents an attack upon women.

4. Operationally, the whole idea of the primal wound is disastrous. Once an adoption has occurred, what good is served by insisting that adoptees are at a higher risk for anything **as a result of separation from their mother**. As J. H. van den Berg writes in <u>Dubious Maternal Affection</u>, "We should realize, however, that there is nothing irrevocable, nothing mathematically certain, in the relation between past and present. A child may become neurotic in the extension of a specific, and in any case too great, ambivalence during childhood. He may just as well grow up perfectly normal. He may even become normal in the process of growing up. Many children with an unfavorable prognosis become normal and productive people without any help at all." And as the Sluckins echo, "Our message to the mother who harbours secret fears, lest she has not been properly bonded to her infant is 'Stop worrying, your anxiety is the result of your acceptance of the bonding doctrine. It was perfectly sensible of you to believe it when no-one knew better; but we now

know that research findings reveal no critical period for maternal bonding, and these findings strongly indicate that maternal attachment – like child-to-adult attachment – develops in most cases slowly but surely.'"

From this critique, it does not follow that I in any way minimize the loss that every birthparent and adoptee experiences when a child is separated through adoption. The loss is real and of great import. It does have lifelong consequences. But to say that adoption is a lifelong process *does not equate* with the idea that the separation of mother and child as a result of a mother placing a child for adoption is a trauma causing a lifelong primal wound, in terms of which almost every behavior and idea of the adoptee can be explained. Further, I do not deny that separation of a mother and father from child through adoption might sometimes, *depending on a complex of other factors,* result in something like a primal wound in the adopted person. Nor do I deny that every adoptee might *to some degree* suffer something like a primal wound. But, if I understand her rightly, Ms. Verrier claims to be offering a theory about the experience of adoption rather than an ad hoc or perhaps *rhetorical* explanation for how separation of mother and child sometimes affects the individuals whom she has counseled in therapy. Instead of offering insights, she is proposing an ideology.

After an adoptive placement occurs, it does very limited good to insist too broadly on the adoption experience as generative of a primal wound. On the part of adoptees and birth parents, it all too often fosters victim status and self-pity, while encouraging adoptive parents to be so sensitive to their children's primal wounds that they become insight oriented quasi therapists who are always trying to understand their children's internal motivation rather than responding to their children with love, firmness, resolve, and human sympathy (as opposed to quasi professional understanding). Too much psychologizing about the burden and wounds of adoption alienates those who have suffered genuine pain and losses from their own psychological resources and spiritual strengths. Too much pathologizing of adoption forgets that every burden can also be a blessing. The psychological spiritual goal is for the two to coexist, with one feeling or idea prevailing for a time and then the other, without either ever being negated or transcended. In other words, one never gets over the losses of adoption but one can in a certain sense get beyond them to a place of forgiveness, understanding, acceptance, hope and even the anger or righteous indignation that fuels effective action rather than self-destructive rage, guilt and ceaseless self-recriminations. To keep both burden and blessing together requires hard-headed realism, philosophical conviction and imaginative scope. To separate them adds to the internal blights that we know as depression and denial.

Given the political and media setbacks occasioned by the Deboer case, adoption reform advocates need to rethink the agenda. Such rethinking is in need of a clear philosophical-psychological comprehension of the issues involved. The primal wound theory is clearly unsatisfactory.

To succeed with reform we need to emphasize two fundamental ideas. One, that every child is better off being raised by his natal parents except in cases of abuse, neglect or through a *choice* made by natal parents who have been genuinely supported in their exploration and exhaustion of all other alternatives. And, two, all people who walk the face of the earth possess the inalienable right to know their history and to meet the man and woman from whom they drew life and breath. These are *principles* upon which adoption reform can build a human, successful, inclusive political and philosophical agenda. In order to assent to these truths, one needs only common sense, or normal human judgement unclouded by self-interest. Because these faculties characterize nearly everyone, adoption reform can be successful, but not if it appears to be identified with what most people perceive to be anti adoption ideology. What adoption reform does not need is a new ideology so sensitive to one element of the adoption experience that it becomes insensitive to all the others. To reduce any human experience to a single explanation inevitably falsifies and thus dehumanizes that experience.

Adoption Rights and Justice

All they need do is to lift up their hearts
And conceive nobler conditions of life,
acquire
The feelings which will give forms to such a
life, and at once
The necessary organs of these will appear
Just as life first put out arms and legs.

–Hugh McDiarmid
"Talking with Five Thousand People in
Edinburgh"

The adoption rights movement has accomplished much. Over the last four decades, the effect in concert of countless private deeds of extraordinary heroism, the eloquence of standard-bearing words, the sweat, the blood, the tears as Churchill might have said, have changed the contours of adoption's psychological, social and, to some lesser extent, legal environment. The "Days of Wonder," as I have called them, with dramatic changes occurring everywhere.

And yet, it can be argued with almost equal clarity and force, that the map has hardly altered at all and where it has it's only at the borders, in the margins, but not in the capitols. With nearly four decades having elapsed since "the adopted first broke silence," open records seem as far away as ever. Whether we talk about TV or the National Enquirer or the editorial pages of most of the country's newspapers, the situation seems unaltered, so that if you ask the proverbial man on the street if he thinks that everyone ought to know the names of his mother and father, he will look at you quizzically and answer, "Yes," but if you then add, "What if it's an adopted child?" the man will likely pause and stutter or simply answer, "No."

So what is to be done? The first response – understandably and justifiably enough – is always MORE. And more does always need to be done if an injustice prevails, whatever the injustice be. But in addition, what needs to be done is to critically examine what it is about the nature of our collective mindset, that tissue of assumptions that is present everywhere, infiltrating and conditioning the very ground of our conceptualizations, and to critically examine the degree and manner in which that mindset creates and is recreated in by adoption reform.

One specific notion that ought to be examined in its influence on the current shape of adoption reform efforts is the idea that the success and credibility of those efforts depends on whether or not it can be proven by personal testimony, supported by exhaustive scientifically analyzed data, that adoptees or birthparents or even adoptive parents themselves are in any way *victims* of adoption. This idea surely has its source in the fact that for at least the last two decades in America in order to make a claim upon the public conscience one has to have first made a claim and been granted victim status. Since it does appear to be the shortest route to media attention and thus effective political action, it is no wonder that adoption reform has often taken this road. It's a road well traveled indeed.

Victimology, which was the term used by Nicholas von Hoffman to first identify and dub the phenomena, has its roots in the victory of the civil rights movement. Because African-Americans were successful in their heroic struggle to keep their eyes on and finally win not the prize but at least a piece of the American pie, (though there remains a large African-American underclass, pumped up with rage and discontent, whose exclusion from the American dream of justice for all remains a raw reality) other groups with grievances to press and wrongs to right have been quick to imitate them.

Two problems arise here. One is that the art and science of victimology, which works according to a three step program of blaming others and then making them feel guilty enough to redress the wrong and ideally offer reparations, has been conceptually outflanked now in the public debate. Victims needs victimizers who, for most groups making a public claim to victim status, have been white males, living or dead, and impressed into the orthodoxy of a politically incorrect curriculum. But now, through the Men's Movement, white males have succeeded in staking a claim to victim status as well. White males are suffering, too, it seems. The conceptual outflanking I referred to is the doctrine of *co-dependency*, which negates the idea of individual responsibility to a large degree. According to the idea of co-dependency, we are all victims now, co-dependent on each other. Wrongs are rooted not in the exploitation of one person or groups by another, but in co-dependency.

The second problem is that the whole idea of *victimology* in the first place is based on a fundamentally flawed interpretation of the psychological-spiritual meaning of the civil rights movement. Rather than being a wrong or a grievance, racism, whether institutionalized and legally enforced or not, is an EVIL. Only moral, spiritual, philosophical language is commensurate with the phenomena itself. To the degree that the civil rights movement has been successful, it may be described as a *victory* in a heroic effort to overcome evil in the world. The struggle was won on the spiritual plane first rather than exclusively the political. And it was won not by blaming whites so that whites would feel bad and guilty enough to do something about it; it was not won by establishing a blame-guilt-reparations psychology between oppressed and oppressors; *it was won* through the example of individual acts, of sublime courage whose spiritual virtue were undeniable, and through the luminous vision and rhetoric of visionary civil rights leaders whose appeal was not to guilt but to JUSTICE. "We demand justice and are prepared to achieve it at whatever sacrifice and cost" is the message that finally won African Americans their basic, spiritually inalienable rights.

Further, unlike the appeal to guilt which often alienates (and even when it is successful leaves the spiritual, philosophic base of personality untouched) the appeal to justice is an appeal to the strength of the spiritual self. It is an appeal to the noblest part of our humanity. The soaring, cadenced glory of Martin Luther King's speeches appealed to justice, to the spiritual core of the self, to the glow of truth written in our heart and then he asked us to contemplate that brightness while lifting our hearts to act in accordance with the truth discovered therein. He asked that we see the justice of his case, the truth of his beliefs and further realize that because when we deny the humanity of another man, woman or child we also deny the humanity in ourselves. Racism corrupts and, therefore, afflicts the racist, too, by contracting the very boundaries of the soul into their least expansive magnanimities.

Open records and open adoption and the full restoration of civil and spiritual rights to the adoptees, the birthparents and the adoptive parents as well, will come, if it is to come, in similar fashion. *It will not* come through anguished voices fixed into the groove of their own individual lament; *it will not* come through the display of wounds; *it will not* come through attacks on other triad members or professionals or the institution itself. *It will not* come through victimology.

Full civil rights for adoptees will come only through a demand for justice; only through an appeal to the spiritual strength and goodness of others which requires a prior heartfelt belief in humanity's basic, essential goodness. And that prior, heartfelt belief requires an overpowering spiritual love for humankind, the spiritual love felt by all great spiritual leaders, by prophets and poets, heroes and bards. It is the spiritual love that Alfred Adler called *gemeinschaftsgefuhl.*

Justice is a spiritual virtue and a philosophical notion. It is alien to the world of social science. The influence of social science has reduced the whole discussion of open adoption and open records to a pointless argument about whether or not birthparents and adoptees are truly victims, or are truly victimized by the old closed adoption system. Is adoption a primal wound? A cumulative trauma? An evil? A disease? Do adoptees who search have more or less self-esteem? Do most searches have positive outcomes? No, say some. Yes, say others; and they have the facts to prove it. To my mind the whole discussion, although relevant and an enrichment of clinical knowledge, is in no way decisive. Adoption reform will not come through a vision clouded and entrapped by identification with a social science methodology.

With regard to open records and open adoptions, it does not matter whether adoption harms or helps, whether it wounds or cures, whether it solves problems or creates them. The essential point is that every human being on the face of the earth has the right to look into the eyes of those from whom they drew life and to whom they gave life and to know their names and stories; that no human law or convention has the right to deny to them this inalienable human right. *It is only just.* And it is my belief, heartfelt as well, that no human being would wish to deny adoptees that right once he can be helped to see the human justice of it. And certainly I do not believe that any adoptive parents (whose love for the child of their heart and kindness is as enduring and ennobling as any love on earth) would deny that right to their adopted children. They least of all would deny their children what is just.

But if they do not see it, it is not because they are blind; it is because their eyes have not yet opened.

Love and respect and understanding are the answer. Not blame and guilt.

*

An Open Letter To The State Legislature

To speak as a professional is something of a burden. To be a professional, to hold a doctorate in psychology, to be licensed as a family therapist, to have published half a dozen books and monographs on adoption, and to hold the position of Director of Counseling at a large adoption agency (all of which I have or have done) means that one is expected to walk and talk like a professional. In other words, pompous and boring.

In speaking out for open records, I hope to be neither. I will not quote studies. As Mr. Jim Gritter has said, "Will studies prove the beauty of a flower?" or do we wait for "studies" before trying to practice the "golden rule?"

Every human being who walks upon the face of the earth has the inalienable right to know the names and faces, and to look into the eyes of those who gave them birth.

In my view, every human being has this right and, as a matter of fact, for most of human history we have known it. Closed records represent a historical aberration. The first sealed records law dates only to 1917 in Minnesota. Other states were slow to follow. Institutionalized secrecy did not become the rule until the 1940's. Open records are the traditional way.

Is the question really, "Do we have the right to open records when so many lives are affected?"

Isn't the true question, "Did we have the right to close them?"

On the basis of a number of years of casework, study, scholarship and writing, it is my heartfelt conviction that secrecy in adoption is always harmful. But even if it were somehow possible to prove, which it definitely is not, that secrecy is helpful, it would not be right.

Only the truth in adoption and the truth about adoption will ever set free those whose lives have been touched by adoption.

To open records now is simply to give justice where justice is due. I urge you, for all of our sakes, to pass the proposed legislation. Open your hearts and open the records.

Family Preservation

Since spirituality is so central to my writings about adoption, it is with some embarrassment that I realize that I have never really approached the term directly.

Clear, however, from the foregoing chapters, is my belief that it is only through an increase in our life in the spirit that we can ever hope to free our hearts from bondage. It is only through spirituality that we can liberate them from what Blake called "mind forged manacles," whose cumulative freight of insecurities and egoism, of material greeds and emotional blockages, prevents us from taking full possession of our inheritance of green pastures and still waters, of peace and justice, of tolerance, freedom, joy and love.

Clear, too, I hope, is my contention that the dominant models – developmental psychology, bonding and attachment theory, psychoanalysis and social scientism – that are used in the field in order to insight the meaning of adoption are themselves, if not exactly suppressive of human spirituality, are nevertheless – how shall I say it? – disadvantageous to the maturation of the spiritual gifts of vision, wisdom and love.

In this last summation, I propose to remedy that flaw.

What is the spirit? Within the context of an essay, I hesitate to say.

For many years, I have believed poetry to be the only medium sufficiently delicate, nuanced, provisional and, most critically, rhythmical enough to express the meaning of spirituality. It is an old teaching in nearly every tradition that as language approaches the condition of spiritual reality, so that it begins to serve as an effective medium for expressions and an articulation of spirituality's most complex, interdependent, heart-breaking and heart-shaking realities, it begins to throb with an ecstatic blur of rhythm. The drum, the blood, the pulse, with their mixing of sensual and spiritual essences, drives the speaker on into an almost supersensual trance. He or she will speak in tongues as it were, the harmonies of rhyme and the intensities of rhythm. The rhythm is both the means of ascent, the invitation to the spirit to come, and also the confirmation that indeed the spirit has come. Since to speak about spirituality requires that we be present to the spirit and the spirit present to us, poetry would seem to represent the only valid vehicle.

But then I chanced upon Robert Duncan's idea that "the essay moves as the poem moves, with the breath," and the example of this very same essay, The Truth and Life of Myth, in which this sentence appears, where the essay does move as the poem moves, alive and pulsing, sensitive and expressive of the most subtle, spiritual discernments.

My method of approach, as always, shall be personal and anecdotal, from which I hope to distill ample insight. This is to be a meditation and excursion more on the model of the great High Romantic poems than of scientific research. As I have tried to establish elsewhere, I believe the truest speech to be the most revealing speech, by which a writer reveals both the nature of the subject he or she explores together with the nature of his or her participation in the subject. In this way, writing is always a voyage in self-discovery.

And finally, so that readers may put away their fear that they are about to be coaxed or hammered by any form of doctrinaire religiosity, just a brief exposition on the context of my use of the word spirituality might be useful here. The context here will be that of a human spirituality that for me has a three-fold source; in the parables and the stories of the Bible; in the visionary tradition of the High Romantic poets; and in phenomenological existentialist philosophy.

As a representative type of this human spirituality, I would adduce the example of Hugh MacDiarmid, who united a visionary, poetic, even prophetic idealism with a warm embrace of our sensual embodied natures, while joining both to a stunning range of practical commitments.

> *And quicken me to the gloriously and terribly*
> *illuminating*
> *Integration of the physical and spiritual til I feel*
> *how easily*
> *I could put my hand gently on the whole round*
> *world.*
> *As on my sweetheart's head and draw it to me.*

How does the spirit move? As is the case with anything essentially human, spirituality begins with a human experience of the spirit. Where and how does one experience the spirit? "Like a thief in the night," says the gospel. "Upon the Wild West Wind," says Shelley. Mary Shelley found it in a thunderstorm when a poetic voice spoke through her to warn the world of the wages of a Frankenstein-like infatuation with technology. More often though, it's in humbler circumstances as with Yeats, *"While upon the shop and street I gazed / my body of a sudden blazed / and for twenty minutes more or less / so great it seemed my tenderness / that I was blessed and could bless."*

The spirit may be experienced anywhere. As Ibn El-Arabi says:

> *My heart is capable of every form:*
> *A cloister for the Monk, a fane for idols,*
> *A pasture for gazelles, the votary's Ka'ba*
> *The tables for the Torah, the Koran.*

Whether on a mountaintop or garden, whether in splendor or in suffering, whether at church or while looking into a glass of wine, the spirit may be experienced anywhere because, as all of the mystics say, the spirit is everywhere.

From whither does it come? *"I asked a child," says an old text, "walking with a candle, 'From where comes that light?'* Instantly he blew it out. *'Tell me where it is gone – and I will tell you where it came from.'"*

For me, the spirit has been everywhere, visiting its beauty upon my heart in a multitude of circumstances, which has occurred sometimes through traditional religious forms but more often through one of those "spots of time" that Wordsworth talks about, where I have found myself in a memory recollected in tranquillity suddenly enraptured by the sense of something greater than humanity present in the world.

I have found the spirit in that old time religion that I knew as a boy in a small East Texas town, where at three o'clock on a Sunday afternoon, with the sky blue and the sun so bright you couldn't look at it directly, we would gather at the river. I would feel the sun on the back of my neck and the warmth through my shirt spreading out across my shoulders. In my memory, now a small shiver of a breeze shakes the thick, green leaves. The air is filled with honeysuckle, the earth, sweet, musk smell and the green erect scent of pine. We're at the riverside, a crowd of us, good church going people here for a baptism. The preacher is my Uncle Bill, a field hand frame and the great, rolling, sonorous, desert scented, Nazareth sounding syllables coming out of his mouth.

The cicadas in the background, now the breeze has settled. We crowd near to the river bank, the creek bank. It's called Kickapoo after an old Indian tribe. The water is rich and brown but clean and clear at the same time. The preacher takes the young girl by the hand. In white dress, she glows with beauty with her golden hair pinned up in back, the white flesh of her long, soft arms brilliant in the sun. He takes her by the hand and with great long, strong, proud strides they enter into the river where they stop and stand waist high in the waters. He says the verses and takes her by the neck with one hand and puts a white cloth over her mouth and plunges her into the water. Quickly, it is over and she rises wet and gorgeous and born again into the new life of the spirit. "Hallelujah's" spread out from us, old men, women mostly, but field hands too and many, many children. Then food comes out and we drink iced tea and fry fish and soak our tongues in watermelon until the moon comes up.

I have found the spirit, too, in the Catholic Mass.

Though a child of the fundamentalist South, I went to a Catholic university, where I would often attend Mass, attracted – attracted by what? Even now, I'm not quite sure. At first, I suppose it was simply curiosity. Finding myself at this little liberal arts college, tucked away in a quiet, high place, at the edge of an immense urban sprawl, I was curious about the religion that made the place so different than anything that I had experienced before. For it was different: it had a contemplative air about it; a genuine respect for learning, and philosophy was so palpable that it hushed footsteps in the halls. Everywhere there were symbols of the spiritual life, from the statues and icons and grottos; to the nuns and priests who smoked and drank, whose manners and wit were elegantly polished, who spoke three languages and were, in every way, so different than the rural preachers that I had known in the small country town where my grandparents lived or the liberal protestant ministers in the suburbs who thundered, to my father's great dismay, the gospel of social action.

The Mass itself was also beautiful and nourished in me a hunger for beauty whose only nourishment until that time had been a high school English class where I discovered Wordsworth and Coleridge, Shelley, Byron and Keats. The vestments and chalice; the solemn cadences and rhythms; the Holy word and readings, induced in me a state of aesthetic rapture that nonetheless bore traces of an authentic spiritual source.

If the Mass nourished my hunger for beauty, it fed as well, through the readings of the Gospel, my need to believe in the timeless power of love which I had first heard from the country preachers and in gospel music floating on the honeysuckle breeze and then found affirmed and celebrated in the High Romantic poets. My own spiritual life, my aspiring efforts to live according to the canons of peace and justice, had become so interwoven with inspiration from the stories of the Old and New Testament that without hearing them on a weekly, and sometimes even daily, basis I would have been as directionless and inert as a rudderless ship on a windless sea.

I have felt the spirit too in other less formally religious ways. I have felt it in the ensorcellments of love and beauty. To Humayra, said the Prophet Muhammed: *Speak to me oh, Humayra, speak and cause to be ensorcelled by your beauty and drawn closer to you, so that the radiance of pure love may enter and transfigure my bodily nature.* Or as Peter Gabriel says, *"In your eyes, the doorway to a thousand churches."*

I have felt it, too, at the edge of death, when in early December we laid my grandfather to his rest, beneath the sky scrubbed blue and bright, beneath an Indian Summer sun — the same Indian Summer sun that had risen there for generations upon my family as they arose each day to the smell of coffee brewed with spring water and the promise of a day of solid, sweat-hard work.

I have felt it, too, in the delight of *homo ludens*, with my son at a soccer tournament, with pavilions of color rising everywhere, the smell of grills and picnics in the air, when, in the pitch of excitement, the soccer ball skims across the dark green grass while behind it, like an archer become his arrow, a young boy flies, the parents shout like a cloud of noise, and then *all suspended* and *then* the shot, the flailing goalie with his outstretched arms and *then* the ball in the net quivering and squirming and *then* the joy of the son and the pride of his father brighten all our eyes.

I have smelled the spirit too in a rain-soaked lily; tasted it in cornbread and iced tea; and saw it move once – delicate, so delicate in the coppery, thrilling weightless flash of a doe, as startled by the golden light laid down by a screen-door opening, she bounded from my grandmother's garden into the summer dark.

Whether occurring through the mediation of traditional religious forms or through the smaller, humbler radiances of ordinary life, what is universal about human spirituality is an overpowering and reassuring "sense" or "intuition," rather than a clear conviction, that in the world there is a greater power present which transcends the merely human and yet is also present within the soul of our humanity, planting its footsteps on our hearts; and, furthermore, that this presence is both good and generous and involved in the human drama. Within the event of every "descent of the dove" or the "eagle" as the native American traditions say, or however our tradition gives to us the vehicle to imagine it, arrives the knowledge that neither the self nor the material, environmental world are their own explanations, but instead depend upon some greater power, so that our being-in-the-world always has the quality of a gift, a miracle, whose very existence is instant by instant successively renewed through an overflowing goodness existing both within and beyond the terms of our humanity.

A philosopher might call this the experience of a radical, but meaningful, contingency.

But to the rest of us, human spirituality might be better described as simply an experience which leaves us touched and shivering and reassured that there is more to human life than meets the eye, or in fact, meets any of the senses, *though it always appears through the senses;* and that this "more" sometimes, perhaps for reasons of its own, or perhaps in response to some absurdity or grace, participates in even the most humdrum, quotidian of lives. *While on the shop and street I gazed. . .*

In adoption, too, I have thrilled to the spirit. Some of these moments I have tried to describe through various vignettes about triad members who through some experience or reflection completed the brightness of their hearts on the wings of spiritual intuition. There was the boy with his eyes swimming in the lamplight who shared his secret that he sometimes felt that he had never been born; the birthmother who slept at night with her arms wrapped tightly around the doll; the infertile man who each year went fishing to think upon the things his boy and he would have done had not the child died at birth; the preacher who discovered his mother, whom he'd idealized, had a child out of wedlock; the hard, strong laborer and the child with eyes that shine; the African American adoptive mother who offered up a prayer, *"Dear Lord, who has blessed my family today with a joy and love that truly is surpassing, bless this woman, too, for though I cannot understand"* – and then she gazed deeply into birthmother's eyes – *"your pain, your grief in having to give away this child. God in His infinite wisdom knows and shares and feels it and, I hope I can feel it someday too. I know he will heal us both. In healing us, heal our child who is not our child at all, but who is His, whom He gives to us because He loves us as we must learn to love one another."*

But rather than these luminous details, what has brought adoption to my mind as a vessel of spirituality is really contemplation of the *gestalt* of the phenomena itself. What is an adoptive family made of, if not biology and genes? Heart and soul can be the only answer. So what is so magical to me about adoption is that what is made *only* out of heart and soul, with no biological kinship or history to ground it, can be so strong and enduring as to cause an ontological transformation. "Invisible connexions are stronger than visible ones," said Heraclitus, as if describing adoption. In the depths of their spirit adoptees truly are twice born, children both of their kind and of strangers' kindness. As Jean Paton writes:

I am one
Who was delivered into adoption,
And it rests on me until I am dust.
It is my name.

I did not know it was adoption
Sped me in such courses.
It did seem to me,
Riding the wind
Of a tumultuous destiny,
That there was laid
Fire in my very bones,
And that the breath of morning

Waited there to cool
This urgent breeding of the soul,
As though flesh never touched

But only dew should wash
These stubborn feet
That trod such eminences
Only a special grant of creation
Did permit to.

Oh, culture could not make it just a one
A many-winged clarion-voiced
Ultimately enduring one!

What a careful phenomenology of the adoptive family also suggests is that all those lofty visionary ideals that would charge us with the task of overcoming all our differences so as to share in one common life, whose only ground are the spiritual virtues of faith and hope and charity, and in terms of whose shared love we assume a new identity, are perhaps not as unrealistic as first they sound for precisely this is what happens through adoption where those who are not bound by anything other than their love and history come together to form a new identity. The rebirth of the adoptee into a new identity is also a rebirth into a new community whose only ground is love. Through adoption, especially in open adoption – where the connection is not built solely on the love that springs up and is sustained on a daily basis between nurturer and child – strangers who are separated by every fate and circumstance, really do come to love each other as themselves, interweaving the beatings of their heart through the formation of a new collective identity, through a new experience of "family" where "family" transcends its ordinary genetic connotation. "Family of Man," Family of adoption: the fact of the *second* proves the possibility of the first.

Adoption truly does foreshadow the way that races and ethnic groups, although estranged for centuries by strife, can, through acceptance and convergence of mutual need and human vulnerability, join into the joy of a common love, a common loyalty, a common life.

Then His brothers and His mother came, and standing outside they sent to Him, calling Him. Then a multitude was sitting around Him; and they said to Him, "Look, Your mother and Your brothers are outside seeking You." But He answered them, saying, "Who is My mother, or My brothers?" And He looked around in the circle at those who sat about Him and said, "Here are My mother and My brothers! For whosoever does the will of God is My sister and My brother and My mother."

Or as Robert Duncan (who was himself an adoptee – how strange the fact that the greatest poet of the last fifty years was adopted has not been noticed) says,

There is no
good a man has in his own things except
it be in the community of every thing;
no nature he has
but in his nature hidden in the heart of the living,
in the great household.
The cosmos will not
dissolve its orders at man's evil.

Here crystallizes the spiritual failure of closed adoption and its connection with other spiritual heresies in the history of humanity where believing in the spirit and the power of the spirit to heal all wounds has become a belief in *only* spirit, a belief that would forsake our common humanity, the flesh and blood of history and especially sexuality. Closed adoption commits the most common form of spiritual evil in its desire to sunder soul and body, spirituality and human sexuality. *But adoption is about sex.* It's about steamy windows and long summer nights. It's about turned-back sheets and undulating bodies. It's about groping and leaks and accidents. And from the other side, the side of the infertile couple: it's about the heart-breaking, void-making, soul bearing realization that something is wrong, that something is not working, that something is not happening that should be happening in the sperm or in the womb. And then it's about the bending back and bending over, the thermometers and jars, the mood swings and medications, the sex by the clock and calendar, the monthly disappointment.

Adoption really starts with menstruation, the great unmentionable monthly flow. On the one side, it's a period missed, and then missed again, as the walls begin to close in on a young woman or a couple, alone and frightened by the life beginning to surge within her. And for the infertile couple: it's the tear-wrapped, shoulder sagging, "what's wrong, honey," downcast disappointment that the flow has started once again.

Like the Grand Inquisitor, closed adoption has so much loved the spirit that it has abandoned the flesh. But the healing of humanity comes only through a spirituality incarnate, a spirituality that, as Denis de Rougemont has said, *"can come to the aid of the flesh and so recover the support of the flesh and let the flesh submit to the spirit and thus recover peace. There lies the way."*

But does closed adoption truly love the spirit? I think not. For behind the fear of the body, history and sex, there always lurks a doubt in the true redemptive power of human spirituality, for to believe in the spirit is to *bear all things, believe all things, hope all things, endure all things because the love of the spirit never fails.* To believe in the spirit is to know that true spirituality can move mountains, that it can withstand all challenges, all defiances and all assaults. It is a fabric that cannot be ripped. In the very opposition to openness, to the past of the flesh and heart in any form, advocates of closed adoption betray their own doubt that the spirit truly can endure all things. They show they doubt the healing power of love. They believe love to be so fragile as to require the artificial protection of the law.

And yet, and yet. . . With the coming of the Christ into the world, there came as well the slaughter of the innocents. . . Matthew 2:11-18 *"And when they were come into the house, they saw the young child with Mary his mother, and fell down, and worshipped him: and when they had opened their treasures, they presented unto him gifts; gold, and frankincense, and myrrh.*

And being warned of God in a dream that they should not return to Herod, they departed into their own country another way. And when they were departed, behold, the angel of the Lord appeareth to Joseph in a dream, saying, 'Arise, and take the young child and his mother, and flee into Egypt; and be thou there until I bring thee word: for Herod will seek the young child to destroy him.' When he arose, he took the young child and his mother by night, and departed into Egypt: And was there until the death of Herod: that it might be fulfilled which was spoken of the Lord by the prophet, saying, 'Out of Egypt have I called my son.' Then Herod, when he saw that he was mocked of the wise men, was exceeding wroth, and sent forth, and slew all the children that were in Bethlehem, and in all the coasts thereof, from two years old and under, according to the time which he had diligently enquired of the wise men. Then was fulfilled that which was spoken by Jere-my the prophet, saying, 'In Ra`ma was there a voice heard, lamentation, and weeping, and great mourning, Rachel weeping for her children, and would not be comforted, because they are not.'" "Hail, Mary full of grace," says Elizabeth, but then she too was pregnant. . . *what would Rachel have said?*

Is adoption worth the tragedy? Must the loss, the pain, the devastation occur? Must there be injuries, trauma and anchorless drift? Are there not alternatives? The logic of my position – the heart, too, has logic, though it is not that of the head – that is to say, my visionary embrace of a definition of adoption that allies it more with a spiritual path than an operation of social engineering now compels me to a position more sympathetic to the family preservation movement whose essential plank is that a parent's union with a child through the rhythm of biological creation is inviolable, so much so that it is worthy of clear legal protection and concerted societal support and subsidy, with the purpose of guarding it from exploitation by more economically privileged infertile couples who ache for a child. In those few cases where parenting is impossible, argue these advocates, legal guardianship, which refuses the notion of a "new" set of parents replacing the old, rather than adoption, is the answer.

Annette Baran and Reuben Pannor in A Time for Sweeping Change wrote, *"We have been active supporters and participants in the adoption reform movement. We believe, now, that it is time to move beyond and address basic issues. Otherwise, we remain an instrument in perpetuating the problem. Each year that we delay, thousands of new adoptees, adoptive parents, and birthparents join the list of the afflicted.*

"What have we, in the adoption reform movement, really been doing the last two decades? It seems to us that if we take off our blinders, we must admit that we have been co-opted into supporting a system that causes pain and lifelong suffering to all the parties involved. A study of the conference programs, the adoption literature, and the media attention clearly points up the direction we have taken. We are all involved in patching up and maintaining a flawed institution. We talk about and offer so called solutions to adoptees, birthparents, and adoptive parents. We try to help them live within the system today as well as tomorrow. Let us now recognize and acknowledge our own vested interest in perpetuating this system.

"A time has come to utilize our knowledge and experience with the past and present to forge a totally new direction for the future. . .

"Relinquishment of children to a new set of parents, is a final, irrevocable act, severing all rights of the birthparents, and must be discontinued. Open adoption, which we helped pioneer, is not a solution to the problem inherent in adoption. Without legal sanction, open adoption is an unenforceable agreement at the

whim of the adoptive parents. Instead, a form of guardianship adoption would be in the best interest of all concerned, with special benefits for the adoptee. It decreases the abandonment, rejection issue and permits the child to know that the birthparents cared but could not raise him."

In a previous book, I rejected the family preservation and legal guardianship idea because of my own emotional reaction to *the horror, the horror* – Marlowe's words are right – of abused and battered children. After one has seen a few cases of real child abuse, one begins to doubt, if not recoil, from any notion of biological kinship that would endow biological connection with some kind of preeminent, moral status. "Like a mother," as in adoption, was better than a mother who wasn't like a mother at all. I realize now both the logical flaw in this position as well as the terrible injustice of simply assuming somehow that a connection exists between parents who would consider placing their child for adoption and parents who physically, emotionally, psychologically, or sexually abuse a child.

To recognize this flaw in my thinking and this bias in my heart was to recognize as well the inauthentic nature of my "understanding" of birthparents. Behind my "sensitivity" there apparently lurked some terrible assumptions. I acknowledge and disclose them now with the hope that my heart and vision can transcend them.

My vision of adoption and what adoption can be said to prove, of what adoption can be said to show about the utter redemptive power of the human heart and the eternal quality of spiritually conceived connections, shows me perhaps a way to believe that the spirit is true enough, strong enough, and at work enough in all our lives to render possible a world where adoption would no longer be needed. It is possible.

The concrete means for achieving this is by means of the philosophy of family preservation, whose first stage is creation of a philosophic theater of discourse consistent with implementation in the social sphere, where it would assume the form of concrete programs for young parents that would allow them to keep their children, to love and raise them into a spiritually rich maturity. The means for doing this are at hand, although implementation requires the most inventive and flexible of programs. But the means are at hand: if, for example, one were to take the total sum of money given in support of adoption agencies throughout the country and were to divide that money equally to provide education, training, support and child care expenses for every birthmother who actually did release a child, the available sum would be considerable, perhaps in the neighborhood of $20,000 or $25,000 per child.

In this context, I think of an adoptive mother, who is truly one of the most honorable, loving and decent women that I have met, who came to a session with her heart and shoulders wrapped with pain and tears. On the night before our session, she and her husband had finally gone for an evening out after having had their dreams and wishes come true two years earlier with the placement of an infant in their arms. Finally, she had been able to let go enough to trust someone else with her baby for a few hours.

That night, after the evening's glow subsided, she had taken the babysitter home, wanting to give her husband a chance to get to bed a little earlier. On the way home, the babysitter had asked her about her daughter – Amy, we shall call her – and whether it was true that Amy was adopted. "Yes," said the mother with a long pause. "Why couldn't her real mother keep her?" went on the babysitter. Biting her lip even at this rather innocent insensitivity, the woman responded, "Because she couldn't afford to give Amy what she needs to have for a chance at life." Another long pause. "Then why didn't you just give her some money?" said the babysitter. "Why did you have to take her baby?"

"I dropped her off without saying anything else," the mother told me. "I know she didn't mean it to be cruel, but afterwards I couldn't go home. I just went and parked beside the lake for an hour and watched the stars and the other people parked and the moon shining on the water and I cried."

It's a terrifically painful truth, a tragic truth, but it is a truth, it is the truth, in a certain way.

To maintain, on the one hand, that a young couple or a young woman is mature enough to make an irreversible decision to place a child for adoption, and, in addition, to describe this act as an essentially altruistic, selfless one that subordinates their or her interest to the best interest of the child; while insisting on the other hand that the mere fact of economic dependence or marginality disqualifies one from the role of parent, truly does make money the bottom line in life. Under any other circumstance, maturity, altruism and the ability to put the child's needs first are the very definition of the good parent.

It also assumes that present living circumstances of someone so mature and altruistic were somehow an indication of future financial failure when in fact quite the opposite is true in that mature, altruistic people who are capable of subordinating their own needs to a larger purpose often succeed quite famously in the work place, if they are not inextinguishably traumatized by loss.

If we are not to totally wrap our tongues in self-serving contradictions, we must also be very cautious with idealizations about the maturity and altruism of birthparents in light of the overwhelming body of family law, which asserts very clearly the preeminence of the natal bond such that it cannot be severed except under the most distressing of circumstances, i.e. severe abuse or neglect. Once a child is a few years of age it becomes very, very difficult to terminate parental rights even when the parents' behavior has been monstrously abusive. So why, one must ask, is it such a simple procedure to terminate those rights, when the child is an infant and the parents are described as mature and altruistic?

The only way to overcome the inconsistency as well as eclipsing the implicit Calvinism that equates personal value with economic worth would be to support adoption only in the case of true orphans or where neglect or abuse has occurred.

But power should not substitute for authority here. Acquisition of power always erodes the authority of vision. The role of professionals ought not to be to dictate other peoples' lives under the cover of speaking in the best interest of the child. In my view, we cannot be so certain about anything in adoption as to either limit or even encroach upon the freedom of young couples and women to place their children with adoptive families. The role of professionals should be to determine their own position with enough cogency and spark to inspire others through their vision and example to a particular course of action. *Though it may be permissible to speak out in the name of God, we ought not to try to stand in for Him (or Her).*

And yet, we must do this without adding further, by thoughtless implications or punitive ideological climate, to the already immense burden of a young couple who, when faced with overwhelming odds that would seem to rob them of a future, elect to place their child. By effects too subtle to ever calibrate a "climate of opinion," which is determined in large part by those who write and speak, will be to some degree internalized by everyone involved in the field.

Too much heart and vitriol poured into anti-adoption sentiments have demoralizing effects on those who do not feel they have a choice, or had one.

It is quite possible and consistent to thunder, for example, against poverty, to work for serious, fundamental economic reform, while also feeding the poor and respecting the fact that, despite its debilitating burden, poverty is sometimes voluntarily chosen, not by choosing poverty itself, but by choosing acts that in this world are certain to lead to poverty. Further, poverty can often be an occasion of spiritual enlightenment and self-transformation. And further still, this position can be sustained while refusing to participate in any way in the stigmatization of the poor.

So, too, with adoption.

For family preservation philosophy to carry with it something more than the "shock of the new," it would need to be contextualized in terms of the following framework.

First, we must recognize that if adoption has victims, so too does it have value, and that this value is essential and enduring, even if for the last fifty years that value has been corrupted by a spiritually unwise philosophy and improper ethical practices. The almost universal employment in all spiritual traditions of the idea of adoption to describe the ideal relationship obtaining between humanity and the divine suggests that there is something intrinsically sublime about the idea, and that in some sense adoptees are "special."

The supreme irony of adoption and the adoptive family is that what its life suggests about the creativity of the spirit and the potentially transforming power of love is that adoption ought not to be necessary. If through the medium of law and social work the spirit can create a new identity defined by love, so working through the same mediums we ought to believe that the love and the spirit are strong enough to enable a family to recreate itself in a form prepared to parent.

Second, we must not oppose family preservation to open adoption; instead, they coexist along a continuum of care. Open adoption has perils. Open adoption has pitfalls. Open adoption is abused. Open adoption is used to exploit birthparents. But not all the time. And not by everyone. And both in its human touch and noble philosophy, it transcends the injustices of the old closed system. The refusal to distinguish between the media pitch of adoption without tears and the treasures of compassion found in cooperative adoption betokens a legal mind trying to win an argument rather than a philosophic sensibility attempting to renew itself in love.

Third, family preservation thought ought not to minimize the supreme difficulties that emerge when children are kept within the extended family system when their parents are unable or unwilling to care for them. By no means is family preservation new. It has always coexisted with adoption. A week's familiarity with an average child guidance center or family therapy clinic is enough to realize that in probably the majority of cases where parents cannot care for their child, it is Grandma, grandparents or some other relative or even friends who assume that role. In other words, some form of family preservation is the choice of all concerned because: it's human; it's natural; it's also spontaneous. But – and here I speak as a therapist with years of experience involved with families in just this kind of situation – such parenting arrangements are in no way a solution. At best, they are only moderately less problematic in terms of discipline, development and identity formation, than is open adoption. Where it is nearly always more difficult is financially. And while money can't buy anyone love, it does buy comfort, security and education, which are not advantages at which we ought to scoff even if in any authentic hierarchy of human values, they rate rather low.

Fourth, the distinction between nature and nurture, genetics and environment, between heritage and parenting is inadequate. Nurture creates its own history, which although of a different kind than biological heritage is not therefore a-historical or meaningless. The spirit has its history as well as the flesh.

Fifth, family preservation advocates must be extremely careful to distinguish their argument from the cliched absurdity of "where there's a will there's a way." Reality is not so atomized. Nor we so much the captains of our fate. Rather, *where there is a collective will there is an individual way, sometimes.* And it is the role of the writer to create that will with new ideals, visions and ardors. Poets are, as Shelley said, the unacknowledged legislators of humankind. Where there is no collective will, and certainly a collective will in support of family preservation has not existed in the past, nor does it exist today, nor is it likely to coalesce tomorrow; an individual way exists only when quickened by sublime, extraordinary heroism.

From this point of view, birthparents, birthmothers who against all odds and advice and facing total isolation have chosen or now choose to parent their children are heroes. That a birthparent does not choose or did not chose to parent a child means that with that single decision in their lives they were not heroes. But after all, who is? Or was? To be too disappointed or bitter at a parent who turns out to be like most other people is not yet to have put away all childish things.

And finally most critically, and yet most painfully, we must not yield in our desire to be as compassionate as possible to the reassuring, but nevertheless, inaccurate cliche that "there are no unwanted children, only unwanted pregnancies." As Shulamith Sha`har says in her exhaustive study, Childhood in the Middle Ages, "The statement that *'there are no unwanted children, only unwanted pregnancies,'* which is over-optimistic, if not sanctimonious, in the context of modern society, is even more so in the medieval context." (See p. 122 and discussion.) To totally remove all socio-economic pressure and incentives to place a child in adoption, even to remove the entire adoption institution itself would not obliterate all instances of placement or abandonment by fathers and mothers. That it would dramatically reduce such separations of parent and child, perhaps even to the point of statistical insignificance, although it would not eliminate them, ought to be an ideal worthy enough. Human nature is such that abandonment would still occur. To keep this point firmly in mind is to ground one's rhetoric in the tenaciously complex soil of humanity.

However, I think it disastrously unwise to stop with only legal guardianship and family preservation, which looks, as our profession always does, for external social solutions for social problems. In my view, the problems of society reflect spiritual disorder. To really believe in the spirit and so to move with the spirit, sustained by its compassionate sanities, into a world where adoption is no longer needed is possible only on the basis of a spiritual revolution that includes a renewal and revisioning of our sexual consciousness and soul. My sense is that if we really trusted sexuality as a vehicle for spiritual revelation, the number of "untimely" or even "unwanted pregnancies" would at the very least diminish.

It may be that adoption, and the need for adoption, is rooted in the larger issue of the relationship of spirituality and sexuality of the soul and the body, and the need for social forms and ethical teachings that arise out of a spiritually true metaphysical intuition about sex. I speak of mystery here, not morality. Lawrence and Yeats, not those who cast the first stone.

Further, in advancing the cause of family preservation, we must not commit the same mistake of spiritual utopianism out of which closed adoption materialized. We must avoid the spiritual evils of fanaticism sapped of all compassion, contentious singularity, humorless rage or the self-righteous indignation that sees the beam in our brother's or sister's eye while ignoring the log in our own. We must heal, not attack, affirm not affront, serve not criticize, shelter and not cast out. And we must be prepared as well to assume responsibility not only for what we mean to say but also for the effect of what we say has on others even when the effects are what we did not intend.

And finally, we cannot simply forget history without forfeiting ourselves, for we are historical creatures, even if, as Joyce says, history is a nightmare from which we are trying to awaken. We must understand the history of adoption, with all its maelstroms and enigmas, while accepting and affirming it as a revelation of the spirit too.

Out of life comes life, out of death comes death, out of the spirit comes spirit, in which life and death, tragedy and love, suffering and joy commingle. Although the history of adoption, as is the history of nearly every adoptee, darkens with suffering, out of that history, too, has come love and joy and an awakening to the spirit. To act, to suffer and to learn, to be transformed and then to transform others with the liberation of one's wisdom: this is the way of the spirit.

Oh, in the days of youth,
Of all torments the most terrible
Not to be like others,
Never to live a single day
Without being painfully reminded
That one is not like others,
Never to be able to run with the crowd,
The pleasure and joy of youth,
Never to be able to abandon oneself freely,
Always, as soon as one would venture on that,
To be reminded of the chains,
The isolation of separateness,
Which with a pain close to despair
Divides one from all that is called
Human life and cheerfulness and joy.
One can, it is true, by the most frightful efforts,
Endeavor to conceal what one at that age
Regards as his disgrace,
That he is not like others.
This may perhaps succeed up to a certain point
But nevertheless the torment is in the heart,
And the success is assured
Only up to a certain point.

With the years, certainly,
This pain disappears more and more,
For in the measure one becomes
More and more spirit.
It is no longer painful
Not to be like the others.
Spirit is just this-
Not to be like the others.

–Hugh MacDiarmid, "Goal"

"His attitude towards woman is the basic point
A man must have thought out to know
Where he honestly stands."

–Hugh McDiarmid

Love Remembered:

A Philosophical Inquiry Into Illegitimacy

The bastard, the illegitimate one, is with us once again. So, too, the unwed mother, hurrying, harassed, turned away from the door. From the right, though not only from the right, a variety of social critics, political and religious voices have joined in blaming the unwed mother and her child for the shape of a society whose distress is crushing the hearts of our cities as well as the hearts of those who dwell in them. To cure these ills, they urge restoration of "family values" and the restructuring of public policy to support them. They wish to restore what they believe to be the traditional stigma of illegitimacy.

In response I think of a time when at a post adoption conference in Austin, Texas, near the river, in the middle of July, I found myself out walking during lunch. The memory flows: pushing out of the blinding Texas heat into the cool, vaulted dark of the college chapel, where once inside the outer door, the dry, sweet resinous smell of burning incense rises up to meet me, while my eyes fall upon a poster that each parishioner must pass before entering into the sanctuary. On it appears an African-American young woman. With head propped up against the wall, she lies upon the cold cement floor of a shelter for the homeless. Her hair disheveled, her faded, flowered dress tattered and torn and wrapped around her almost like a blanket, and with eyes wide and marble white with fear, she has curled into a fetal position so as to better protect the infant, innocent with sleep, whom she holds in her arms. Under the image appear these words from the book of Matthew:

> *"Then they will answer him, saying, 'Lord, when did we see You hungry or thirsty or a stranger or naked or sick or in prison, and did not minister to you?'*
>
> *"Then he will answer them, saying, 'Assuredly, I say to you, inasmuch as you did not do it to one of the least of these, you did not do it to Me.'"*

The "family values" point of view sends down deep historical roots in the adoption community. More than a generation ago at just the time when both its value and viability seemed shaky, David Kirk explained how the adoptive placement of children has been used to reinforce the two parent nuclear family as ideal.

Kirk writes: "Adoptive kinship, having been grafted onto the mainstream family system and intended to simulate it in all ways, became thus a kind of symbolic bulwark against the progressive weakening of the family as institution. While this was intended for the benefit of adoptees and adopters alike, it has become increasingly apparent that the adopted – partially at least beneficiaries of the arrangement – have grievances, chiefly relating to their inability as adults to command the same freedom of information as that given to other adults in this society." (H. David Kirk, Adoptive Kinship, Ben-Simon Publications, p. 140-141.)

Even so, for many in the adoption world, "adoption" and "family values" continue to equate.

But the problem with presenting the family as the solution is that it is a double edged sword. Just as social critics from the right are now blaming all mayhem and malaise on the breakdown of the family, not so long ago did men and women of the left blame the family for every social evil. With some plausibility, Bukharin, Reich, and later Cooper and Laing, etc., condemned the family as the factory of fascism. "A vassal factory," said Reich. The storm trooper and the swastika, the collapse of Europe into the dust and rubble of two world wars originated, according to these critics, in the traditional family with its isolation, intolerance and dogmatic religion, its patriarchal structures and authoritarian attitudes, its suppression of women and of sex, its joyless, punitive childraising practices, and subordination of individual rights to the order of the group, and all imposed with an overt air of self-righteous moral superiority.

But even if we're willing to swing a two-edged sword, explanations that seek to account for social disorder in terms of the family are unsatisfactory because the family itself does not belong to the order of absolute values. From a philosophic point of view, "family" is not a matter of what Paul Tillich called "ultimate concern." When family does become an absolute, humanity diminishes. The most sublime of the great Greek tragedies, the Orestia concerns this issue, as does Romeo and Juliet among numberless examples.

When it is the family rather than justice that determines guilt and punishment; when it is the family rather than love that determines interpersonal relations; when it is the continuity of the family that we worship over all other values; when the family determines our purposes and controls our fate; when it is to our families rather than to ourselves that we be true, then we soon forfeit our souls. When we have not family, we still have many things including the liberations of justice, love, truth, beauty, etc.

Relatives are only relatives; they are not absolutes.

According to both logic and metaphysics, the lower cannot explain the higher. Therefore no arrangement or mathematics of the family can explain the individual.

In their assumption that much of our behavior can be explained in terms of the family, conservative social critics are not alone. On the same dais they could be joined by systems theorist, family therapist, recovery guru, all of whom share the "family is all" philosophy. But if the family is neither supreme metaphor nor absolute value, then, to paraphrase the unhappy woman in the Don Henley song, who has learned that "every form of refuge has its price," how did things get this crazy?

They got this crazy as they always do, that is, on the basis of a philosophical mistake, that though innocent, perhaps, in source, nevertheless once made, soon acquired a superstructure of ideas, interests and institutions with a very strong stake in perpetuation of the error.

At least in the consulting room, whose influence runs much deeper than we usually imagine, the enthronement of the family as absolute value, supreme metaphor and most enduring influence, probably dates back to the gestalt discovery that the whole differs from its parts. I say "differs" because this difference does constitute the genuine intellectual breakthrough, for although there are multiple foreshadowings in past philosophy of the gestalt idea, it was never so precisely perceived and consistently established.

Sadly, however, and with tenacious ramifications, this "difference" was wrongly interpreted in terms of a mathematically based construct of "greater than or less than" so that it is in the form of "the whole is greater than its parts" that the gestalt discovery has been integrated into contemporary disciplines.

From a philosophical point of view, however, whose insights are securely anchored in a metaphysical doctrine of manifold states of being, neither the whole nor the system nor the family is greater than any of its parts anymore than a nation is greater that its citizens.

Sometimes this "different" reality of the system or family may appear to be more important than other realities, but this depends upon attribution of value, which is always an expression of individual reality.

But it does not follow from this position that the family exists only as an idea, a mere name or *nomina,* without extramental referent or reality. Rather, just as we exist in soul, spirit and body, in history and eternity, as individuals and as participants in various unities, so we exist in families as well. But to weigh the relative value of each of these modalities requires an individual act of value attribution, which implies that from a metaphysical viewpoint the personhood of individuals remains the fundamental reality, prior in the realm of values too all other modalities, while existentially we all coexist in a variety of simultaneous, interdependent ways.

As often occurs, the celebration of "family values," where family is synonymous with the two parent nuclear family, converges with denunciations of the unwed mother and the bastard. In her book, <u>Illegitimacy: An Examination of Bastardy</u>, Jenny Teichman writes: "The point of legitimate/

illegitimate distinction is not to cause suffering; rather, it has to do with certain widespread human aims connected with the regulation of sexual activities and of population." (Jenny Teichman, Illegitimacy An Examination of Bastardy, Cornell University Press, p. 4-5.) But this is quite in error, for the fact is that the purpose of the stigma of illegitimacy has been to reinforce a particular psycho-social-sexual code by punishing those who defy it.

In this chapter, I want to inquire into the idea of illegitimacy with the intention of revealing the motivations that create both the idea and the stigma, which, as we shall see, are not interchangeable.

Why fathom such an obscure matter when the overt sexual nature of the theme risks controversy, invites sensationalism, repulses or intimidates. *Because it matters to adoption.* If the "family values" agenda is successful in restoring the stigma of illegitimacy, I fear that, if this stigma is vicious enough, then young women will be even more disposed to place their faith and renewed dependence on those who offer the illusory kindness of a closed adoption where the stigma may be erased while the mother is freed to live her life as if she'd never sinned, never been stained, never broke the taboo, as if she'd never had the child at all.

Such a development I would regard as catastrophic for all concerned, but irretrievably for the child who will be denied the basic anchorage in life and love that comes from continuity with the history of one's parent, family, people, clan.

That so many advocates of closed adoption do double duty as champions of "family values" should come as no surprise. The second surely serves the interests of the first.

Further, here at the outset, I should wish to discard as relevant for my purpose the various sociological investigations of illegitimacy. The prototypical social scientist commences study with a definition of "illegitimacy" derived from Western history, philosophy and forms of consciousness and then "finds" this idea operative in other cultures. In this way, the social scientist can "prove" the universality of the notion. For example: "No matter how varied the definitions and rituals of marriage and kinship structure, virtually all societies distinguish between legitimacy and illegitimacy of birth and apply penalties to unmarried parents and, in many cases, to illegitimate children. Illegitimacy, therefore, involves the absence of legitimacy, but the most important aspect is not a 'formal law,' but the recognition by the social group of the rights and responsibilities of parenthood." (Shirley Foster Hartley, <u>Illegitimacy</u>, University of California Press, p. 3.)

This won't do. First, the idea of illegitimacy cannot be established as a universal so long as any single exception exists. Exceptions do exist. One instance: illegitimacy did not exist under Brehon law which once governed most of Ireland, Scotland, England and Wales. Hamish Henderson assembles some of the evidence: "Much fascinating information about the sexual mores of medieval Celtic society is to be found in Kenneth Nicholls' <u>Gaelic and Gaelicized Ireland in the Middle Ages</u>. The rights enjoyed by women under Brehon law — which continued to be operative in most parts of Ireland until the seventeenth century, although 'officially' terminated by the Statutes of Kilkenny in 1366 – would be the envy of women's libbers in many parts of the world in 1980. Women had the right of independent property ownership, could divorce and remarry with ease, and could be practitioners of the arts and sciences if they so desired. 'There was no such thing as an illegitimate child; a mother had simply to 'name' the child and if it was son, he would inherit part of his father's property. Marriage was one of the keys to Irish women's independence, based as it was upon a complex series of property relationships which did not automatically involve property transfer from women to men.' Nicholls tells us that 'down to the end of the old order in 1603, what could be called Celtic secular marriage remained the norm in Ireland. . . Christian matrimony was no more than the rare exception grafted on to this system." (Edited by Robert O'Driscoll, The Celtic Consciousness, George Braziller, Inc., p. 259.) Modern states, too, have sometimes dispensed with it: Sweden, New Zealand, etc.

Second, less obviously but more critically, illegitimacy concerns sex whose mysteries are intimate and individual.

Human sexuality is too magical with excitement, too varied in norm, too vulnerable in expression, too private in performance, too indescribable in sensation and altogether too obscurely human in its contents to ever yield its essence to sociological inquiry.

After all, men and women often live and love together for a lifetime, share their secrets and their sorrows, their beds and baths, without ever really sharing their most private, embarrassing sexual fears and fantasies. It is somewhat implausible to believe that they would reveal them to a stranger or a questionnaire. When data is gathered by such research, it ought to be qualified as information conveyed without the kind of personal trust, connection and exchange of mutual vulnerability that seems to be the condition, the sine qua non, of revelation of the vibrant, living presences of our sexual imagination.

*

What is bastardy? Who is the bastard? The illegitimate one. The outcast, the scapegoat, the villain. Does illegitimacy truly carry with it such an ancient stigma as some now would suggest?

Not so, for much of our shared past. During most of Western history, bastardy has served only as a legal determination for the purpose of maintaining property intact while also providing for an orderly transmission from one generation to another. Illegitimacy described the legal status of someone fathered out of wedlock when he appeared in court in the attempt to claim his father's property the same way that a plaintiff describes the legal status of someone when he appears before the court to press a lawsuit. For so long, as no means existed for establishing paternity beyond a legal doubt, society required some way to distinguish between legal heirs, among whom the property would be divided, and illegal or illegitimate heirs. The emphasis fell on the second of these two words.

To the degree that a society revolves around individual property rights, some grounds had to be found for denying endless claims on personal property. Without such means, property could never be secure. To own property would mean to spend most of one's time in court protecting it from putative "heirs." In the sense of conception and birth outside of legal marriage, illegitimacy met this need.

When the French Revolution dethroned the ancient regime, one of the many motives compelling the dispossessed was the cry, "There are no bastards in France." But over just this issue of inheritance the revolutionary lawmakers foundered when they attempted to abolish illegitimacy. Jenny Teichman explains: "Bastards were to have the same rights of inheritance against fathers as legitimate children. However, a bastard making a claim against an estate had to offer proof that he was indeed the son of the man whose estate it had been; proof had to consist in writings by the father or in evidence of a bastard son's having been maintained by him 'under the name of paternity' during his lifetime. The same requirements for proof of parentage were needed if a bastard made a claim against the estate of his mother. Subject to proof of parentage, bastards were to have the same rights of inheritance against collateral kin as those held by legitimate people. Bastards were to have a right of maintenance by their fathers if the father was unmarried, but a married father needed to pay only one-third of the sum that an unmarried man would have to pay." (Jenny Teichman, Illegitimacy: An Examination of Bastardy, Cornell University Press, p. 154-155.)

However, these laws were never implemented. By the time of Napoleon, the reaction of privilege against liberty had so ferociously set in that the situation of illegitimacy worsened. The laws grew harsher; application, stiffer; penalties, more severe. The stigma that had been absent in the past emerged.

In the medieval world, whose social order was deeply rooted in religious values, illegitimacy bore scant stigma. Jean Meyer says, "No stigma attached to the word 'bastard' which was, on the contrary, a title to be proudly emblazoned on one's crest. In the mid-sixteenth century the Lord of Gouberville, a country gentleman of Cotentin, thought it quite natural to bring up his bastards at home together with his legitimate children. Sexual licence outside marriage was by no means confined to the nobility but was present in all sections of society, though it varied between classes, between regions and over the centuries. The religious laxity of the late middle ages was reflected in general moral laxity, but with the Reformation and the Catholic renaissance came a reaffirmation of the sanctity of marriage culminating in the austerity of the Jansenists and of the *Catechisme de Nantes* (1689) in which

Mesnard, its author, laid down that 'conjugal chastity must keep lust and passion within bounds.'" (Quoted in Ferdinand Mount, The Subversive Family An Alternative History Of Love and Marriage, Jonathan Cape, p. 132-133.)

To some degree, such tolerance survived even into modern times: Alan Macfarlane explains: "A brief survey of seventeenth-century English sources tends to give the impression that bastardy, though its ascription might be libellous, was not greatly disapproved of, as long as the child was maintained. Thus one vicar described how a neighbor had a maid who produced four successive bastards, 'yet because she was a good work woman he kept her still.' Gervase Holles recorded, more with fond indulgence than indignation or horror, that one of his uncles was very enamoured of women and begat several illegitimate children. It seems quite likely that sympathy with the plight of the mother and general tolerance of bastardy as a frailty, but not a sin, continued at least until the nineteenth century. Even in that century there are indications of such tolerance in two of the classical accounts of rural life at that time, *Lark Rise to Candleford* and *Forty Years in a Moorland Parish.* It is possible that the situation was similar to that observed in other societies, where there may be a scandal at the time, but afterwards the child, mother and father are accepted back into normal social relations and the affair does not cause shame." (Quoted in Ferdinand Mount, The Subversive Family An Alternative History Of Love and Marriage, Jonathan Cape, p. 132.)

To thieve a bit from Gertrude Stein: the law is the law is the law. And a determination called illegitimacy has been the law, so as to guarantee the rights and continuity of property. But until only a few centuries ago, the law was just that: the law. The law portioned out reality only when reality was in dispute. Justice is another name for reassertion or for discovery of the real when what is real is in dispute. But beyond these fairly narrowly conceived confines it was the law of the heart and soul and spirit that was applicable. In other words, although the law applied to persons, the meaning of personhood transcended the law. Although a bastard could not be an heir without first being *legally* legitimized, to not be an heir did not signify that one was not a son or a daughter whose parents kept them close in their prayers, their fears and their hearts. All echoed this response. It was not so much that bastards were beautiful, as the bumper sticker says, but that sons and daughters were thought beautiful. If they sprang to being from the wrong side of the bed, so to speak, it disqualified them only from the inheritance of parental property, not from the devotion of parental love.

By the eighteenth century, however, issues of illegitimacy, female sexuality, reproductive freedom, contraception, abortion, etc. had become a blank slate incurring a variety of male fantasies and projections whose sum effect was both to create the stigma of illegitimacy and to desexualize women. Angus McLaren writes: "Thus the medical literature depicts a change from the sexually active woman of the seventeenth century to the passionless creature of the nineteenth. The reasons for this are still under debate. Some writers have suggested that the rise of evangelical religion was responsible for the new stress on women's chastity, decorum and purity. Others have argued that doctors rather than priests played a key role in counselling moderation – that purity and suspicion of sexuality were exploited by physicians in order to enhance their positions as counsellors and confessors. Still others have suggested that the emergence of a new economic view of the world that lauded thrift, prudence and self-control necessarily influenced in a negative fashion sensual enjoyments. . .

". . .In a remarkably similar fashion medical scientists appear to have turned the later eighteenth-century discussion of procreation to the purposes of bolstering a new, middle-class image of the respectable, asexual female. The notion of aggressive, female sexuality did not disappear but would henceforth be associated by medical men only with working-class women. Doctors in this way contributed to the effort made on a variety of fronts by the middle classes to elaborate new social and sexual roles to differentiate their enlightened lives from the unthinking, hedonistic existences of both the upper and lower orders." (Angus McLaren, Reproductive Rituals, Methuen & Co. Ltd., p. 27-28.)

Why and how did such a change occur? The shift in attitude reflects a more fundamental shift in spiritual philosophical attitude which occurred in the seventeenth century. As Denis de Rougemont observes: "For all, the whole lot of us, lead our lives of civilized people quite without suspecting that those lives are being led amid a strictly insensate confusion of religions never completely dead, and seldom altogether understood and practised; of moral teachings which once upon a time were mutually exclusive but now are superimposed upon one another, or else combined in the background of our elementary behaviour; of unsuspected complexes which, because unsuspected, are the more active; and of instincts inherited less from some animal nature than from customs entirely forgotten, customs which have turned into mental furrows or scars, that are unconscious, and, on that account, easily confused with instinct. They were once upon a time either cruel artifices, sacred rites or magical gestures, or again profound disciplines elaborated by some kind of mysticism remote alike in time and space." (Denis de Rougemont, Love in the Western World, Harper Torchbooks, p. 115.)

What de Rougemont claims proves especially true when the associations are with sex, because human sexuality and human spirituality are so intimately bound.

During the seventeenth century – on November 20, 1620, to be precise – the battle of White Mountain occurred where two forms of metaphysics, of religion, culture and spirituality, which had long struggled for preeminence in the West, took the field against each other. On the one side, marching under the lion banners of the Winter King and Queen of Bohemia, were the traditions of a chivalric, mystical Protestantism, of what Ezra Pound called the "Spirit of Romance" and the historian, Francis Yates, the "Rosicrucian Enlightenment," while on the other side advanced the forces of reaction and counter-reformation. In the tradition of romance, whose soul cannot be confined to any single religion, time or culture, but instead has surfaced as Celtic Church, in the popular medieval Cult of Mary and the Saints, in mystical Cabala, troubadours, Italian and English Renaissance, neoplatonism, romantic poetry, etc. the feminine is revered, cherished, worshipped as saint, Mary, Queen of Heaven, Blessed Virgin, Mother of God, Sophia. But at the White Mountain, this tradition was decisively destroyed. Never again would it flourish as the basis of a living culture. Deprived of its exoteric base, it would degenerate into the mere "esotericism" of private philosophy, personal mysticism, syncretic cult or anachronistic ceremonial whose main attraction was to personal dispositions already estranged from the mainstream instead of mature belief. Since for the opposing forces woman and the feminine have always been a source of ambivalence and anxiety, a presence feared, elusive, enigmatic, interchangeable at its worst moments with the witch, a temptress, a seductress, ultimately itself an illusion since, from a spiritual viewpoint, it is always on earth as it is in heaven, and from the heaven of the anti-romantic spirit, whether it appears in rigid religious dogma, counter-reformation imperialism, scientism, materialism, empiricism, economicism, the female is always banned. With no divine archetype to bless and sanction her living reality, the mystery of the feminine soon becomes the blank slate of the female on which men were free to inscribe their own projections. As soon as man ceased to be subject to a Divine Woman, real living women became subject to less than divine men.

Behind all this, these forces of reaction: a fear of sex. And out of fear, a desire to control human sexuality. The men of power so recoiled from sex because sexuality, with its volatility and vulnerability, is always the great barrier to the totalitarian ambition that wishes to control every dimension of human life. Sex and love are overpowering, overwhelming, mystical, extraordinary human realities.

Sex is fire in the heart, a flowing light, a mystical passion. Experienced at the base of one's being with the imperishable, unconditional substance of one's heart, while at the same time disrupting all social, racial, class, ethnic and religious lines, *sexual attraction overrides all else.* To be in love is to be a lover before any other role. "I have greater joy in one look or word from you, my lady, than in universal knowledge," said Goethe. Love creates its own world, its own space, its own language, its own calendar. Sometimes destroying virtue, it creates it too, so that the lover is with lunatic and poet all compact. Make love not war, but the lover is the greatest warrior in defense of his Beloved. Love is blind. A god. An immortal, imperishable, indestructible substance. The force through the green fuse drives. The glittering stream. Tristran and Iseult. Paulo and Francesca. Romeo and Juliet. "When a man loves a woman, there ain't nothing he won't do. He'll turn his back on his best friend, if he puts her down. He'll give up all his comforts. He'll sleep out in the rain. If that's the way she says it is supposed to be."

If sexual passion overwhelms all class and culture lines, so for many men and women it exalts consciousness. Sex not only thrills and warms, satisfies and procreates, but, when accepted as a revelation of the spirit, it also focuses, intensifies, liberates and ultimately transforms. In the ardor and exultation of sexual passion, consciousness transcends its ordinary limitations, which are so paltry, petty and ego bound, to participate for a moment in the metaphysical realm. As Yeats says, "*. . .,I take / That stillness for a theme / Where his heart my heart did seem / And both adrift on the miraculous stream / Where — wrote a learned astrologer / The Zodiac is changed into a sphere.*" (Edited by M. L. Rosenthal, Selected Poems and Two Plays of William Butler Yeats, Collier Books, p. 150.) Or another Irish poet, *"Behind our eyelids a landscape opens, a violet horizon pilgrims labour across, a sky of colours that change, explode a fantail of stars the mental lightning of sex illuminating the walls of the skull; a floating pleasure dome."* (Edited by Frank Ormsby, The Long Embrace: Twentieth Century Irish Love Poems, p. 84.) As religious mystics often employ sexual metaphors to evoke the mystic state, so sexual ecstasy is sometimes a mystic state whereby the soul experiences the divinity. Sexual passion can generate the rapture.

Sexual passion, the liberation in the soul of the great God Eros, the "fearful enchanter" and "mighty warrior" as Plato calls him, is one of the occasions in which we participate in the abundance and agape of the divine life.

Thus sexual passion not only threatens the stability of society, it also relativizes its importance through a revelation of a more primary, primordial level of existence. Through love and passion, the sexual and spiritual combine to undermine the sociological. For politicians and social scientists this scandalizes. Truly, sexual passion discloses that there are more things in heaven and earth than are dreamt of in our philosophy, our politics and our social sciences.

So wherever the desire exists to compromise human freedom, it is sexuality that suffers the most sustained, visceral attack. Passion becomes pornographic. However, since sex is such an intimate, numinous, overpowering circumstance, it is impossible to control. But if unlawful sex cannot be proscribed, what can be proscribed: what can be vilified, condemned and ostracized is the issue of unlawful sex; that is, the child. The tool of such proscription is the stigma of illegitimacy. The child becomes a bastard. Further, through the evidence of birth, the mother too can be incriminated. Thus, with the absence of some reliable contraception, the possible consequence of proscribed forms of sexual activity would appear to be so devastating as to discourage acting on desire. In this way, the stigma of illegitimacy serves as an effective limitation of female sexual freedom.

The stigma is reinforced in the following three ways.

First, sexual sin is isolated from the continuum of our humanity, so as to seem the quintessence of human evil.

It's not only sexual sin that is evil, instead sex is evil. And then evil is sex. Eve, the temptress. The apple, a woman's soft flesh.

With the tut-tut toryism that mars her otherwise interesting work, Jenny Teichman both describes and defends the practice. "From time to time one can hear people deploring the common man's equation of morals and morality with sexual morality. It is fashionable among moral philosophers to assert that sexual morality is only a small part of morality *per se.* But this view point ignores the historical fact that the major religions have always shown an extremely lively interest in all questions of sexual morality, so that teachings on sexual matters actually form a very large portion of moral teachings *per se.* The interest is by no means dead, nor even slackening: for every Roman Catholic sermon preached against bank robbery there must be several thousand preached against contraception.

"Why is this? Should we attribute it to the rise of capitalism? The phenomenon is too ancient and too widespread. Is it caused by the kinkiness of the celibate clergy? The phenomenon is not confined to them. Is the explanation Freudian, relating to the 'dark, irrational forces' which allegedly dominate all mankind? The reason, whatever it is, is certainly very ancient." (Jenny Teichman, Illegitimacy An Examination of Bastardy, Cornell University Press, p. 149-150.)

That the Gospels and the Christ as He moved among the people, cooking fish for them, sharing their bread and their hardships, so consistently spurn this unlovely, moralizing view, suggests that Nietzsche was perhaps only accurate with his aphorism "that there has been only one Christian in the world, and He died on the Cross." The parable of the adulteress and the first stone precisely contradicts the "common sense" morality championed by Ms. Teichman. And what about the Woman at the Well?

What Ms. Teichman names as "the common man's equation" of morality with sexual morality represents not common sense but the cast the first stone morality of Pharisee and Sadducee; that is, the insufferable, opinionated, legalistic, conformist element in the soul whose blindness darkens the poetic-spiritual splendor of the visionary healing of the gospel.

Further, one might note, that the common man typically applies this equation to the common woman, but not to himself.

Second, the social order separates women from a chance to earn a living and pay their bills and thus decide on how and with whom they want to live. "The general rule in the past was that a legitimate child belonged by law or custom to its father. In ancient times a woman could not be the guardian of her own children – first, because she was herself under guardianship of some kind all her life and, second, because quite usually a married woman's right to own property or real estate was either restricted or non-existent, making it difficult or impossible for her to support a child." (Jenny Teichman, Illegitimacy An Examination of Bastardy, Cornell University Press, p. 40.)

Third, the institution of adoption materializes as a socially accepted means for relegitimizing the child. But by functioning as a guilt producing mechanism which strengthens the social-sexual code, adoption dispossesses women from their natural liberties. When a woman finds herself pregnant outside of wedlock, she is immobilized by a double bind situation. If she elects to keep her child, she condemns both herself and her issue to a life of stigma and impoverishment, which means she cannot help but suffer from the distress of guilt. But, on the other hand, if the child is surrendered – the word is apt – she will suffer too as she cannot help but worry with the fear and feeling that she has abandoned her child to the kindness of strangers behind whose smile lies at worst a void and at best the whimsicality of fate. In either case, she is discouraged from any further "license," any further attempt to challenge the social-sexual order with her freedom and desire.

So much has been written about secondary infertility in birthparents, even where there is no physical cause, that one has to wonder if the symptom can't be explained on the grounds that somehow the "life-force" (meant here in the broadest of ways) has been voluntarily withdrawn from sexual communion in some way.

And if someone refuses sex, they are not likely to have children either. In any case, the sum effect of adoption is to reinforce the social code where the limits to sexual freedom are very clear.

For illegitimacy to retain a stigma, these three factors must remain in force. Today, however, the relevance of all three factors has eroded.

Whether it means we're going to the dogs or not, society as a whole no longer restricts by either penalty of law or climate of opinion the unconstrained exercise of sexual freedom in whatever way an individual chooses. Part of the attack on illegitimacy is to eliminate this freedom as well. But as it is, people remain free to act on their own desire as they see fit.

It is probably worth pointing out here that sexual freedom is not exactly new. In every culture and every soul, the prude and the libertine, license and rigidity are in conflict.

Both custom and law have transcended the prejudice that any reasons suffice for denying women equal rights and opportunities in the workplace. Where disparities exist, as among African American and other minority youth, where young women find it impossible to attain a standard of living that can support a child, we generally accept this to be a result of discrimination or at the very least an absence of opportunity rather than reflecting anything essential about the nature of women. Certainly, we do not believe the disparity warrants legal sanction.

We have finally accepted that adoption cannot relegitimize a child in the sense of negating the fact of birth and heritage. While two ways may exist to come into a family, through birth or adoption, there are not two ways to come into the world: that happens only through birth. The life of an adoptee begins at birth not adoption despite the fraudulent creation of a new birth certificate, which is perhaps the last vestige of soon to be bygone injustice.

Hence, the stigma of illegitimacy ought to have gone with the wind, rejoining our own age to the traditional sanities of most of those who have walked this planet before us. And, as a matter of fact, it has, though a broadly based movement seems to be coalescing, whose goal is to restore the stigma.

To acquiesce to such a harsh and needless relabeling at a time when existing social forces no longer make it in any way either desirable or necessary, and with an understanding of how our own tradition rejects such labeling, is to acquiesce as well to a spiritual-philosophical-political agenda whose heart hates women, spurns sex, limits love, and casts out eros from the pantheon of presences whose souls are our emotions. And to do this without acknowledging that this agenda is the cause of the stigma in contrast to believing it to be somehow divinely ordained is to dissemble.

God will have to work in mysterious ways indeed to redeem mankind by making women suffer and by suffering not the little children, red and yellow, black and white, legitimate and bastard, to come unto Him with equal status.

*

By those who excoriate the unwed Mom and her illegitimate progeny, it is sometimes maintained that the disappearance of any stigma to illegitimacy maims fathers as well, turning them into useless, ineffectual Fisher Kings with no essential role to play in the lives of children.

Well, yes and no. Yes, but only if we choose to confine the role of the father to that of Mr. Cosby or Mr. Cleaver, the traditional head of the household in a two parent nuclear family where father's role is as provider. This is the father who brings home the bacon, mows the yard and sleeps on the couch while watching TV. This is fatherhood as Dagwood.

When an unwed mother elects to keep her child, as opposed to placing it for adoption, the father as provider is absent. But this is not synonymous with saying that the child has no father, because he does. Any child, every child has a father who lives in his smile, his looks, his steps, his aptitudes, his genetic and biological heritage. This is the father who, whether present or not, will live in a young boy's or young girl's dreams. Moreover, it does not equate with saying that children of single mothers will have no men in their lives, because undoubtedly they will. A friend, an uncle, a teacher, a coach, a grandfather, etc., will likely take an interest, will bear that child, as Robert Bly has said, in his heart. But, because our society is so afflicted with the idea that a child belongs to a parent as does a piece of personal property, on which a kind of no trespassing sign is posted, too much participation by such role models violates the norm. Others will want to know just why and what is the interest in the boy or the girl, often, by the tone of their voice or the arch of their eyebrows implying that such interest is abnormal. Too much help, interest or guidance arouses the specter of child abuse, so that most men in the past have shied away from such personal involvements.

In many respects, though more difficult to precisely locate, to attach too much stigma to illegitimacy, is as much an attack on men and their freedom as it is an attack on women.

Children require more men in their lives than only their father, whose role, of course, is vital but not exclusive, and men need more inspirations for themselves, more opportunities for stateliness and splendor, more occasions for accomplishment, in terms of heroic adventure, poetic inspiration, erotic ardor, classical friendship, universal learning, prophetic passion, mystic rapture, chivalric display, and the craftsman's timeless patient labor, than is available when a man chooses to confine himself and his identity to that of father as provider.

By such visions, men coax glory from their hearts.

And children and youth need more opportunities for such men to share their love and their lives, their wisdom and their skill, their temper and their training. When the generations join and share their daily lives only through paternity, only through the father as provider, we all lose out. The solution is not new "earth" fathers – more sensitive, more caring, more involved. The solution is more "fathers," the older generation, for every child; a council of elders sharing responsibility for the younger. The last thing we need is a generation of overinvolved, overprotective fathers.

In such a composition of society, we find the traditional way. Never prior to this day have fathers been confined to the role of provider; never before have men been limited to the role of father; and never before has so much been expected of fathers. The few who do accept this role are suffering. One man cannot carry so heavy a responsibility as the complete, nurturing, disciplining instruction and formation of a young person's soul. In the past, they weren't expected to. Shulamith Shahar here describes the role of the medieval father in the education and parenting of his son. "Didactic writers asserted that the main function of mothers was to rear their sons to the age of 7. In fact, many of those designated for knighthood were separated from their mothers at the age of 7-9. In Gottfried of Strasburg's *Tristan*, the eponymous hero is raised with great love and tenderness by an adoptive mother. At the age of 7, he is forced to leave her, and, according to the author, at the peak of his joyful development, and on the threshold of the spring of his years, anxiety begins to gnaw at his heart. The blossoms of his joy wither and the most beautiful stage in his life lies behind him. Contrary to the advice of authors of didactic works, when children were parted from their mothers, it was not their fathers who undertook their upbringing and vocational training. They were despatched to the courts of other nobles to be educated: to a paternal uncle, a maternal uncle (who was usually of higher social status than the father), a friend of the father or his seigneur, who were often also the child's godparents. In both literature and life, only the eldest sons of great nobles were educated at home, usually with other children and young boys, sons of the father's vassals or friends, and only those who stayed at home remained in close contact with their mothers. Many noblemen acknowledged their bastard sons, reared and educated them at home or sent them, like their legitimate sons, to be raised by other noblemen." (Shulamith Shahar, Childhood In The Middle Ages, Routledge, p. 209.)

So many of the horrors, pains and desperate straits of loneliness that we are busy laying at the doorstep of the unwed mother are problems whose source can be overcome, not by anything so regressive and archaic as reattachment of the stigma of the bastard to children whose only crime was to be born, but by men, all men, not just those whose name will be passed on to another generation, assuming responsibilities toward children as fosterers, mentors, soul friends, spiritual directors, etc. Or just someone to hang out with, to follow around and from whom to learn.

All men bear responsibility for all children, not just fathers for their sons.

The lore is rich; the tradition strong; the paradigms are many. Mentor (Telemachus); William Marshall (Richard Lion-Heart); Sam Fathers (Ike McCaslin); Mr. Miyagi (The Karate Kid).

*

In the last story in Go Down Moses, Faulkner's epic novel about heroism, family, patrimony and love, Ike McCaslin, the hero who has become an old man now, has gone to the woods perhaps for the last time.

On the first morning after breakfast, the other men, including Roth Edmonds, Ike's nephew, a dark, brooding man, leave the camp to hunt, leaving Ike behind in the tent, breathing gently and peacefully so that they think he's still asleep. Ike listens to them go.

Suddenly, the tent flap opens and something jars his cot. It is Roth who tells the old man that a messenger might come for Roth this morning. *"If she does,"* he says, *"tell her no and give her this."*

Roth drops an envelope on the cot. When Ike picks it up, he feels it full of banknotes.

Before Roth is even out of sight, the old man hears an approaching boat and then a young woman comes into the camp and into the tent. She wears a man's hat and rain slicker.

Ike fumbles for the envelope. *"Here. Take it,"* he says. *"Take it,"* and then he becomes aware of her look, a look fixed on his face, with, as Faulkner says, *"that immersed contemplation, that bottomless and intent candor, of a child."*

"You're Uncle Isaac," she said.

"Yes," he said. "But never mind that. Here. Take it. He said to tell you, No." She looked at the envelope, then she took it. It was sealed and bore no superscription. Nevertheless, even after she glanced at the front of it, he watched her hold it in the one

free hand and tear the corner off with her teeth and manage to rip it open and tilt the neat sheaf of bound notes onto the blanket without even glancing at them and look into the empty envelope and take the edge between her teeth and tear it completely open before she crumpled and dropped it.

"That's just money," she said.

"What did you expect? What else did you expect? You have known him long enough or at least often enough to have got that child, and you dont know him any better than that?"

"Not very often. Not very long. Just that week here last fall, and in January he sent for me and we went West, to New Mexico. We were there six weeks, where I could at least sleep in the same apartment where I cooked for him and looked after his clothes—"

"But not marriage," he said. "Not marriage. He didn't promise you that. Don't lie to me. He didn't have to."

"No. He didn't have to. I didn't ask him to. I knew what I was doing. I knew that to begin with, long before honor I imagine he called it told him the time had come to tell me in so many words what his code I suppose he would call it would forbid him forever to do. And we agreed. Then we agreed again before he left New Mexico, to make sure. That that would be all of it. I believed him. No, I dont mean that; I mean I believed myself. I wasn't even listening to him anymore by then because by that time it had been a long time since he had anything else to tell me for me to have to hear. By then I wasn't even listening enough to ask him to please stop talking. I was listening to myself. And I believed it. I must have believed it. I dont see how I could have helped but believed it, because he was gone then as we had agreed and he didn't write as we had agreed, just the money came to the bank in Vicksburg in my name but coming

from nobody as we had agreed. So I must have believed it. I even wrote him last month to make sure again and the letter came back unopened and I was sure. So I left the hospital and rented myself a room to live in until the deer season opened so I could make sure myself and I was waiting beside the road yesterday when your car passed and he saw me and so I was sure."

"Then what do you want?" he said. "What do you want? What do you expect?"

For a while longer, they talked, this woman standing, holding a baby, and the old man sitting, while outside the murmuring rain. They talked of family, of the past, of the interconnections of their lives. And then Ike realizes that this woman, this woman who is carrying a child blood kin to him, is black. As his shock subsides, he reaches up to touch the child. . .
He drew the hand back beneath the blanket again: he said harshly now: "It's a boy, I reckon. They usually are, except that one that was its own mother too."

"Yes," she said. "It's a boy." She stood for a moment longer, looking at him. Just for an instant her free hand moved as though she were about to lift the edge of the raincoat away from the child's face. But she did not. She turned again when once more he said "Wait" and moved beneath the blanket.

"Turn your back," he said. "I am going to get up. I aint got my pants on." Then he could not get up. He sat in the huddled blanket, shaking, while again she turned and looked down at him in dark interrogation. "There," he said harshly, in the thin and shaking old man's voice. "On the nail there. The tent-pole."

"What?" she said.

"The horn!" he said harshly. "The horn." She went and got it, thrust the money into the slicker's side pocket as if it were a rag, a soiled handkerchief, and lifted down the horn, the one which General Compson had left him in his will, covered with the unbroken skin from a buck's shank and bound with silver.

"What?" she said.

"It's his. Take it."

"Oh," she said. "Yes. Thank you."

"Yes," he said, harshly, rapidly, but not so harsh now and soon not harsh at all but just rapid, urgent, until he knew that his voice was running away with him and he had neither intended it nor could stop it: "That's right. Go back North. Marry: a man in your own race. That's the only salvation for you — for a while yet, maybe a long while yet. We will have to wait. Marry a black man. You are young, handsome, almost white; you could find a black man who would see in you what it was you saw in him, who would ask nothing of you and expect less and get even still less than that, if it's revenge you want. Then you will forget all this, forget it ever happened, that he ever existed —" until he could stop it at last and did, sitting there in his huddle of blankets during the instant when, without moving at all, she blazed silently down at him. Then that was gone too. She stood in the gleaming and still dripping slicker, looking quietly down at him from under the sodden hat.

"Old man," she said, "have you lived so long and forgotten so much that you dont remember anything you ever knew or felt or even heard about love?" (William Faulkner, Go Down Moses, The Modern Library, p. 358-363.)

In matters of love, of sex, of pregnancy, of illegitimacy, of adoption, for too long in this country, we've forgotten about love. We need to start remembering.

*

Adoption Loss & the Comfort of Kinship

So much has been written about adoption and loss that one hesitates to speak for fear of belaboring the obvious. But so much has been written about adoption and loss because the adoption experience involves so much loss, and so many different kinds of loss with so many subtle reverberations throughout the psyche.

In this brief note, I want to comment on one particular kind of loss, that as I work with more adult adoptees who have completed a search and whose days now are calming into the colors of life's early and late afternoon seems to me of fundamental importance. To name, bear and be at peace with this loss may be a condition for ultimate healing.

The only way I can evoke it is through a memory – the memory of myself as a boy sitting alongside my grandfather in a pick up truck when he suddenly pulled over to the side of the road. We got out and tramping through the underbrush, our steps occasionally cushioned by pine needles, we walked about twenty yards into the East Texas woods until we came to a clearing.

The day wore cold and overcast. We stood at the edge of the clearing for a moment where tall bare trees stretched out over us. Through them one could glimpse the silver gray clouds racing through the sky. The wind was high and made that cool hollow rushing sound that the wind will sometimes make as it skates unhindered across tall winter grass.

"This is the old place boy," my grandfather said and pointed to the remains of a chimney not too far from where we stood.

It indeed was the old place. It was where my family had settled in the middle part of the nineteenth century, built a house, sunk a well, added a barn, pens for the stock, planted a garden. In 1912 it burned and, as my grandfather told me the story as he'd been told the story, for he wasn't there that day, I felt it, felt the panic in blue eyes that though shaded by a hat or perhaps a bonnet that day were just like mine, as quick to tears, as quick to anger. I felt those eyes peering out of mine now, eyes riding in on the smoke until finding the source, the fire blazing up, logs collapsing into it... "the barn, they say was the first to go. They still don't know what started it..." and then the loud cries, the ringing of the bell, the brothers coming running, the stock bolting, the dogs barking, moiling underfoot, the buckets flashing from hand to hand, but to no avail, and then the house roof catching, the wall of heat pushing back, and then the ground still hot and black and smoking beneath a moon washed miserable night.

Was this a sort of mystical illumination? I have no idea. It faded very quickly. But whether real in a metaphysical sense or simply the product of a young boy's overactive and very impressionable imagination, it left me with an unshakable belief that my family, all those fierce, unfriendly gazes and tall brows and dark blue eyes that stare down at me from so many old portraits and out of so many old photographs, my great-great and great grandparents, the uncles, the aunts, the cousins are somehow all alive in me and I somehow alive in them, that as the Psalmist says about the deity, before I was they knew me, dreamt me, prepared a way, bestowed an ageless blessing.

What this belief has nourished in my heart is what I would like to call the *comfort of kinship*. To be and feel inextricably interconnected, to maintain a sense that we are watched over and cared about by those who have come and gone on before us, to believe that not only here in this life but through the generations the circle is unbroken yields a profound sense of comfort.

In many mythologies as well as in the testimony of those who have survived death or near death experiences, it is an ancestor or family members who come to welcome the departed at the end of that long tunnel that leads to the other side. I recall my sister saying to me once, as she bent over a kitchen sink washing the dinner dishes how she took comfort, so much so that fear of death had lost some of it sting, in the idea that my grandfather would be there to greet her on the other side when she died.

That comfort took on powerful importance a few months later as I watched her rocking on one of those rotating hospital beds, her back, shoulder and leg broken after a near fatal auto accident. She survived, but those moments, when in stunned, wordless grief I stood over her hospital bed were softened slightly by remembering her words and remembering her faith that the circle is unbroken through life, through death.

This sense of being intimately and personally one with one's family, both living and dead, is celebrated by the Catholic Church in the idea of the community of the saints. I have found it described both as a mystical, actual experience, where the ghosts loom near, and as a philosophical conviction in a dozen texts.

I have also found the comfort of kinship described in the writings of the gifted poet and birthparent, Mary Anne Cohen. In her beautiful collection of poems dedicated to exploration of the adoption experience, she begins the work with a tribute to her grandmother:

Irish Maid ... For my grandmother
Anne Devlin Manning

I have never scrubbed
someone else's floor
I rarely scrub my own
I have grown
in the generation that
reaped the rewards
of immigrant women on their knees
soapy rags or rosaries
in their rough hands

Annie crossed bleak western sea
in steerage
out of bloody Belfast
city of perpetual defeat

Annie left her home
for America of
"No Irish Needs Apply"
except
to scrub the floors
dump the slops
braid the hair
of those who could afford

maids and cooks and butlers
and nurses for their babies

Annie came
to the mansions of Long Island
steep backstairs, room
in the garrett beneath
slate-hot roof, above
the rooms of cool silk
protestant ladies,
                    and she met

John with blue eyes, thick black hair
John from Galway, who took care
                    of horses

They were married in Glen Cove,
St. Patrick's church
in weak winter sun of the first
month of this century
with only the priest
and friends
to mark the day

Annie had
six sons, two daughters
Two died before
their second year
Michael, and little Anne–but
everyone she knew
had some who died

she prayed, lit candles, and went
back to work, dry-eyed, because
there were more at home to feed,
and people worse off...

Annie and John
said the Rosary out loud,
with the family
every Saturday night
Annie fed the bums on her street
and the kids, and when
she gave a party,
the upstairs parlor floor
shook all night
with Irish dancing

Annie lived "Down Dublin"
Morristown's tough Irish slum
where genteel people
wouldn't come
she died
before my birth–when I asked
what she died of, my father said
"she just wore out."

I do not scrub
other people's floors
I do not know
my babies dying of poverty
with no time off to grieve
I never say my grandmother, but
I know

Stone courage, plain stews,
strong hands
laughter up backstairs, dancing
at wakes, grieving alone, Fire
in Belfast streets–my bones
Remember.

While later in the same volume she writes:

Annie

who crossed the sea
from Belfast to Brooklyn
maid for the mansions
of Millionaire's Row
She died
before my birth
she is with me
always
her gentleness
lives on

That the poet begins the work in this way is significant.

I find it difficult, even frightening, to imagine what it would be like to lose this comfort, to have no clearing in the woods to take my children, as I did take them, for the first time, the day of my grandfather's funeral, a warm, Indian Summer day, with wild flowers unseasonably blooming. Of course, as a nation of immigrants, all of us have to some degree lost this comfort, especially so for African-Americans who came to this country in chains and in a nightmare instead of in possession of a dream as did most of our other forefathers.

We know to change one's country takes a powerful toll, but can one ever change one's skin, one's flesh and blood, one's family? I think not. Through one lifetime perhaps. But what is one lifetime in light of eternity? Blood will tell, or rather blood should tell – should tell a story of those who walked like us, who talked like us, who brought us forth from the passion of their living. And when blood does not tell, the silence is hollow and stony.

One place where the comfort of kinship will probably never be found is in the autobiography of an adoptee.

As a result of their "placement" – how thin and faithless seems the word when reflecting on all its ultimate significance – adoptees lose this comfort of kinship or at least I think they feel and fear they do. *Where are their sacred places? On what ground do they step to reconnect with their lineage? Who watches over them? Who else is there in the house or at the sickbed when illness threatens or that final time draws near? Who comes to meet them on the other side?*

(Perhaps the terrible grief felt by birthmothers may lie not only in their loss, like the Trojan Women, of a child to uncontrollable forces, but also in their knowledge, carried to the heart, that whether through coercion and collusion of others or through an act of understandable self-preservation, they have broken what cannot be broken, the family bond and thus deprived their child of a comfort that they still possess.)

I'm speaking here in a spiritual and psychological rather than a religious sense. I don't mean to imply that I don't think that God watches over us, or the angels or the saints, or that the Being of Light described in those 'after death' testimonials is Christ. In fact, I do think that. But I also think in addition to the certainty of faith and the consolation of philosophy, there is something called the comfort of kinship, the comfort of belonging to a family that transcends the generations, the comfort of having ancestors whose love and connection to us death cannot erase. I think it is why most of us want to be buried with our families.

This comfort assumes a special meaning at times of emotional and physical crisis. It is when one feels most alone that one has most need of kinship. As we approach any great human trial or tribulation, we all have a need to believe not only that others like us have been there before and triumphed or at least survived these circumstances but that we are connected to them and they to us. And the evidence of humankind is that they are there, watching, guiding, caring, at times even defying the normal laws of the universe to reach out and lend a hand.

I have a friend who every winter talks about walking fifty miles through the Hill Country in Texas where his people come from. "Why?" I ask him. He gazes back over a bottle of wine. "I want to talk to my fathers," he answers.

Another friend who lost a son while he was still a young man shares what comfort she takes from knowing that he is buried, back in the country, in a family plot, where his departed kin can watch over him.

Of all the losses that adoptees suffer, I wonder if this loss is not the most significant precisely because it is something that adoptees often don't realize they are missing. In this way it is unlike separation from a mother or father and therefore, the loss of being raised by them. When adoptees become pregnant or begin to raise a family of their own, it becomes clear very quickly what precisely has been missed and how much has been lost through their separation from their own parents. In contrast, before one needs the comfort of the past, of kinship, of connection with the ancestors, one has to experience genuine tragedy, one needs to have tasted some of the bitterness of life as well as its savor. One needs a certain maturity of vision to realize how much richer and more rooted our life is when we can enjoy a sense that our ancestors are alive in us and we in them. When an adoptee does grow wise and rich enough with life, only then does he or she truly suffer the loss of comfort of kinship. Only then do they begin to ask those questions about where is their sacred place and who will come to meet them at death. And because there is no sacred place and because they cannot be sure who will come to meet them they must confront and bear this loss and speak to the ghosts who through this human act of adoption have also abandoned them.

I think it was this loss that most grieved the single person who has done the most to re-open adoption both in a literal sense and in the larger, more encompassing sense of reopening adoption to the emotions of the heart and eternals of the spirit. I mean Jean Paton, to whom we all owe a personal debt for her courage and her eloquence.

In her classic book *Orphan Voyage*, she describes the final act of her search, the act that once completed permitted her to say, it is finished. Completion, healing, reunion, whatever we may choose to call it, came not in the embrace and acceptance from her birthmother, not from acknowledgment from her birthfather. No, it came only when she journeyed to sit before her grandfather's portrait and summon his ghost. The act does not rejoin her to the dead. That cannot be. From the illegitimate, she knows, the dead, like the living, may have averted their gaze. For her there will be no comfort of kinship, *ever*. Search and reunion may recover continuity with the past but not the comfort that this continuity provides when it remains unbroken. But still she must speak. Here, in imagination, she addresses her father who is also gone, about her talk with that proud, imperious, mysterious old man.

> "Well, Father, my childlessness has broken your line, insofar as it descended into me. Had I known whose it was, perhaps I would have been less careless. Perhaps I would have had a child, or children; and at least I would have recognized these Celtic stirrings as matters to be

known and dealt with, plumbed and lived. I talked with my friends, told them the pieces, and they said: 'Why, His father must have been so-and-so!'

"At least his name was not Smith; also, it was historical, and I was able to personify him. But you, my father, who fumbled with your life, you with your 'laughing eyes,' perhaps because your father was too much for you, well, he was not quite too much for me after all this time. I was old enough, seared enough, ready at last to look him in the eye.

"Of course I could not speak to him any more than to you. But his traces were clear and solid. It was not necessary to scrape around in directories and employment lists to find him. No, he left epitaphs, his self, his things, his expressiveness—all where anyone could see them if they but came.

"I went to the Northwest and I looked at them. I put my hands upon his old office table, scrutinized with understanding the titles in his library, and I looked straight behind his portrait eyes. And perhaps he knew I had come, in my name and in the name of my father-after eighty years."

The final act of healing for Jean Paton, as it probably is for all adoptees, was not to build a bridge but to look across a chasm, which, for adoptees, no bridge can ever span, the chasm which separates the living from the dead, the living from the long dead, the ghosts, the spirits thronging, the eyes that perhaps still look with love and grieve that what once was wished and worked for never came to be, and then to speak and though one hears no answer, to believe that, perhaps, one was heard.

". . .anyone who seriously intends to become a philosopher must 'once in his life' withdraw into himself and attempt, within himself, to overthrow and build anew all the sciences that, up to then, he has been accepting. Philosophy -- wisdom. . . -- is the philosophizer's quite personal affair. . ."

Edmund Husserl
Cartesian Mediations, p. 2

"What is so marked about American social science is the degree to which it is modeled on the natural rather than the historical sciences. . .

"The distinctive character of American social science has necessarily had a profound effect on social practice and social thought in the United States. A historical world is a humanly created one. It is composed of people, institutions, practices, and languages that are created by the circumstances of human experience and sustained by structures of power. History can be used to achieve a critical understanding of historical experience and allows us to change the social structures that shape it. In contrast, the models of the social world that have dominated American social science in the twentieth century invite us to look through history to a presumably natural process beneath."

Dorothy Ross, The Origins of American Social Science,
Cambridge University Press, 1991.

Social Science/ Social Service

A Personal Affair:

Social Science & Adoption

This morning, while still abuzz with coffee, which perhaps made me a trifle more combative than usual, I sat through a presentation by a distinguished social scientist. I say "distinguished" because she holds an academic rank at a decent university and has published widely, including in the prestigious Child Welfare Journal, although in fact her career is young. Clearly, she's bright, industrious, successful.

After a few opening remarks, she details her methodology and data, and the conclusions she has drawn, which, she describes as "tentative." Complete, exhaustive corroboration must await collection and analysis of further data which is already underway.

The whole exercise is funded by a myriad of grant resources.

With her colleague, whose academic position is with an even more prestigious university than her own, she has been researching *open adoption*, a field in which I as an "adoption professional," as we say, take a professional interest.

In compiling her data, she has employed the principle tool of social science research, the questionnaire.

Puzzling over the elaborate charts and graphs and scale analyses and sample questions, most of whose literal meaning entirely eludes me, I raise my hand to ask a little more about her "data base" and subjects. Leafing through the pages, I ask, "Do you have a gender ratio on the subjects who participated in the research?" Afraid that maybe I used the wrong word, I quickly add, "Who exactly answered this questionnaire, more men or women?"

"Yes," she says, though she seems a little edgy so that I think perhaps I've hit on something, "the subjects who actually responded to the questionnaire were about 90% female."

"Let me get this straight," I respond. "This research consists of a questionnaire, made up largely by academicians, that was sent out only to adoptive parents and the majority of the ones who did respond were women? So, if I understand you correctly, the conclusions that you draw are based on what about 150 adoptive mothers, most of whom live in California (that information was on the handout) and who took the time to answer a lengthy questionnaire, have to say about open adoption?"

The look that flashes across her face and on everyone else's face immediately makes it perfectly clear that I have overstepped my bounds. After a furtive glance across the room, I realize that I had better not say any more unless my goal is to be thought rude at best and a crackpot at worst. It's not so much that other professionals present are willing to defend the research. Later, less pointed questions convince me that, at least on some level, most of them are as skeptical as I am. But suddenly, I am aware of the controlling force of an unstated code, which hovers above the room as unmistakably as a smoke signal, that forbids such a challenge to emanate from anyone other than another social scientist, which it is clear, as Bob Dylan might have said, "ain't me babe."

The lecture resumes; concludes. Questions come from the floor. Handouts circulate. We shuffle out the door.

Later that day I find myself trying to convince an agency board member of the wisdom and justice of open adoption and open records. "But you don't have the data to support that," he says, while shaking his head vigorously with his hand raised in a gesture verging on contempt. "I simply can't support something so radical when you can't give me any data or any persuasive research to support your. . . (and here he pauses and aggressively cocks an eyebrow) *opinion.*" "But my experience. . .," I rejoin. "Oh, that's just hearsay," he interrupts and this time I am dismissed.

The stars kindling in the evening sky find me bewildered, beleaguered, furious, exhausted. "If Christ were to appear today," I think smugly, "and wanted to be taken seriously, he couldn't say, 'I am the Truth and the Light.' He would have to say, 'I am the Data and the Results of the Research.' Perhaps then he'd get a hearing."

Truly, it does puzzle me, the respect in the adoption field for the social sciences – indeed the reverence for a mode of knowledge that is neither decisive nor definitive by any properly philosophic criteria. And yet, ironically, despite such high regard, the actual results of social science research only sporadically determine either policy or practice, unless, that is, it can be conscripted to rationalize a position whose motives and antecedents are not remotely connected to a "survey of the scientific literature."

So what explains the respect, the reverence? Does social science deserve it? Should social science research be our guide in adoption? And if not, why not? And if we believe that social science does constitute a reliable consistent model, then what accounts for the fact that the results of social science research do not more decisively affect adoption practice.

In what follows, I wish to explore these questions. But I do so with the stated objective of challenging the idea that social science, no matter how sophisticated the methodology, no matter how exhaustive the data, no matter how brilliant and mathematically precise the analysis, can ever serve as any kind of guide in matters of the heart and soul, which, to me, adoption definitely is.

Second, I wish to show how the ostensible respect for social science among adoption professionals conceals a form of collusion between sociology and social work, between the academy and the agency, that maintains them both in business to the detriment of the clients that adoption ought to serve.

I do so with only one qualification, that being to exempt social scientists themselves from my critique. In fact, to my mind, a number of sociologists – one thinks at once of Professor David Kirk whose genius is simply monumental – have made authoritative, irreplaceable contributions to the adoption field, but each has done so not as a result of, but in spite of, or *in trotz dem*, as Paul Tillich might have said their "scientific methodology." The insights have ignited as a result of the virtues and vigors of the intellect and heart rather than as an outcome of research.

*

"Like aestheticism, scientism was a response to the modernist historical crisis, an effort to make the achievement of science an end in itself and thereby to find order amid historical flux. It was also the result of a long-standing commitment perennially deferred, an effort to make good on the positivist claim that only natural science provided certain knowledge and conferred the power of prediction and control. With science now defined by its method, scientism demanded that the requirements of natural scientific method dominate the practice of social science."

Dorothy Ross, The Origins of American Social Science,
Cambridge University Press, 1991, p. 390

In order to evaluate the value of social science to adoption, we first must inquire into the scientific model itself. In brief, we must ask, "What is science?"

During this century scientific method and the scientific attitude have been philosophically examined by a variety of thinkers from multiple perspectives. Works of singular importance would be Edmund Husserl's The Crisis of European Sciences and Transcendental Phenomenology; Heidegger's What is a Thing; Merleau-Ponty's The Phenomenology of Perception; Rene' Guenon's The Reign of Quantity; Gadamer's Truth and Method; Norwood Hanson's Patterns of Discovery: An Inquiry Into The Conceptual Foundations of Modern Science; Edwin Burtt's The Metaphysical Foundations of Modern Physical Science; and Robert Romanyshyn's Psychological Life: From Science to Metaphor.

As is the case with every discipline, that is, every consistent system of thought, science originates in our shared experience of the world. But whereas the ordinary man with his ordinary perception perceives in reality a world of difference, distinctness, uniqueness, and values, science begins with the intuition of a world of sameness, of identity existing beneath or behind the constantly changing flux of appearances.

Imagine yourself in a grove, in a wild orchard say. It is morning. The sun has just come up and sparkles on the dew and on the tall grass and on the fruits, apples, peaches, plums and pears which hang heavy from the branches through whose dark, shadowy greenery of leaves golden beams of sunlight topple. Now, whereas you as an ordinary man or woman might see "things," our prototypical scientist, *insofar as he is a scientist and not an ordinary man,* would perceive not *things* full of goodness and beauty, but *objects,* defined by their chemical and elemental properties existing within a neutral space time continuum and governed by immutable laws. If an apple fell on his head, so to speak, he wouldn't pick it up and taste its shivery radiance; instead the theory of gravity might occur to him as it did to Newton.

Considered in itself, this world of "sameness" displays an extraordinary beauty, so much so that one may imagine the scientist as a young man who, lying at the edge of a pool one late summer evening, catches in the surface of the pool a silvery reflection of the stars wheeling up above in their slow procession across the vivid deep, dark blue vault of the summer sky. (Most of Newton's discoveries did occur during the long idleness of a brilliant young man's summer.) For a scientist it is as if this "heaven" with its beauty, its timeless unchanging immutable laws, existed here on this plane of reality just behind the surface of appearance. For this reason, perhaps, astronomy, the study of the laws of the heavens, was the first science of which we have any record and the one for which a young child, bursting with curiosity and aflame with the desire to know and understand the world in which he lives, will show an utmost fascination. The archetypal pose of the scientist in art and literature is the scientist, Copernicus, gazing at the heavens.

As the world of difference corresponds with *quality,* so the world of sameness, the world of science, corresponds with *quantity.* Mathematics serves as the perfect instrument to express this quantifiable universe. In phenomenological literature, the attitude of science is often described as having *quantified* and *mathematicized* the reality. And with mathematics emerges the possibility of prediction and with prediction comes control.

Let us return to our wild orchard. Having purged our eye of the sultry seductiveness of appearances, we now see only *objects,* masses of anatomy occupying space and time. As objects located in space and time, they are absolutely comparable. By resolving them into numbers, their very mass may be purged away; so that instead of "objects," we may now contemplate them as *mathematically intelligible structures,* as counters or punctuations in a mathematical equation whose neutrality is such as to be the ideal instrument for expressing the universe of "sameness" where everything – man, woman, child, tree, plant, polished stone, flowing river, sun, moon, and stars – is ultimately identical.

We might say then that it is the work and miracle of the scientific imagination to transform the "thing" that is the term of our ordinary, conventional perception, or what is called perception in the "natural attitude," from *a packet of splendor* into a *pocket of mass* and finally into a *punctuation of a mathematical equation.*

Through this transformation much is lost of course but much is gained. First consider what is gained.

From a philosophic perspective what is gained at first is truth. The scientific imagination expresses truth. On one level of being, in one modality of our existence, we are all identical. Dust to dust, ashes to ashes, as the theologians say, which becomes in the system of scientific discourse, atoms to atoms, quarks to quarks. Further, the truth shines forth as beauty. So science attains both to truth and beauty. But there is more as well: through the ability to express this world of sameness and mathematics, science offers *predictability* and *power* as well.

Back to our orchard. Let us say that our stroller now decides to create a farm. With charts and graphs, slide rules and tables, computers and programs designed for data analysis, he tallies all. Tracking the performance of each vine and tree over several years, he de-forests, prunes, irrigates, replants, analyzes, grafts, harvests and hybrids until his land becomes immensely profitable. (The quantification of reality makes money possible as well.) He's certainly very satisfied with science and all that it's made possible, while his consumers are very satisfied with him.

So far, so good. But here the trouble starts. To continue with our farmer: so successful is his farm, that he hungers to expand it into the neighboring woodlands which he has come to discover are also ripe and fertile. Prior to the amazing success of his farm, he has paid very little attention to the "wilderness" around him except to eye it warily and to occasionally fight it back when its exfoliating growth threatened to encroach upon his farm. He was perfectly prepared to give it over to the poets and lovers who would linger beside its still waters or in the warmth of its tall and fragrant grass. After all, he had first come upon the orchard with love and poetry in his heart, too. But that was before he saw – how shall we say – the possibilities latent. So our farmer begins to talk about *wilderness reclamation* and before too long his greed has grown so great that he drops the word wilderness as well, because that would be too much of an concession to the autonomous right of the trees and stones to exist, so he now will speak only of "undeveloped land."

So, too, with modern science, the science of Copernicus, Galileo and Descartes and the science that, although more or less discarded by contemporary physics, continues to ground the "social sciences." What modern science forgets is its own origin, the original act of abstraction that created it, and therefore, its own relativity to other modes of knowledge that respond and articulate the qualitative modalities of existence.

Again back to our orchard, when it was still an orchard and not "undeveloped land." Consider what must be momentarily suppressed in order for two apples to be compared and ultimately, when resolved into mathematical language, equated with two other fruits from our symbolic orchard.

What is lost is the luster of the orchard as it appears. What is lost is the sensual plentitude of the phenomenal world, the world as it is given in ordinary experience. Gone is the hushed and tranquil silence; the color splashed pageantry of vision; the luscious taste of the fruit; the golden surfaces and textures; no dew wet wild aroma; no anchored fragrance made lovely by the tracings of the wind. Absent too is the living, breathing human body, the *lived body* in phenomenology, the very principle of individuality, the gift the angels envy, to which this phenomenal world appears. To examine the phenomenal world from a scientific model you must in a fashion close your eyes, retract your tongue, curl back your fingers, etc., so as to focus on things as mere envelopes of matter inside of or behind which is the "true" reality. And when the body disappears so, too, do passion and poetry, eros and ecstasy, history and the heart, together with all those distinctive modes of knowledge – empathy, intuition, inspiration, imagination, emotion and common sense, and above all, love – which are traditionally associated with the body. The orchard disappears to be replaced by a diagram, map and formula while we forget that the advance of scientific knowledge is precisely and exclusively *that*: the advance of scientific knowledge rather than an advance of human knowledge, of knowledge about anything essentially human. Certainly, to reduce the orchard to its one mode of quantifiable reality is an immeasurable impoverishment of existential density, dignity and richness.

Science and the scientific method become problematic at the moment they forget their origin in a specific act of vision or ideation which establishes them as an authentic but relative mode of knowledge. Science and the scientific method become *destructive* at the moment that this amnesia is compounded with the arrogance that equates scientific truth with Truth itself, so that all other avenues to truth from philosophy to poetry to mysticism to common sense are viewed as either second-class knowledge or anti-science. Being both qualitative and quantitative, reality is simply too multiform to ever be reduced to a single vision and language.

Regrettably this has been the history of modern science until scientists themselves from Schrodinger to Bohr to Einstein returned it to its source; but even more regrettably it remains the history of modern social science. This is especially a tragedy, for insofar as body, heart, soul and spirit, in which we all are absolutely unique, constitute the "subject" of any discipline, the scientific mode of thought must be rejected as inadequate. And body, soul, heart and spirit are the subjects of social sciences. The scientific mode of study has access only to those elements of human being in which we are all absolutely alike. Of course, on some levels we are alike, but not on those that are constitutive of our humanity. What is measurable about humanity is never as important as what is in and of its very essence immeasurable. And as Heraclitus said, "So deep is the soul that one can never take its measure no matter how hard one tries."

So then as Blake said, "May God us keep / from single vision / and Newton's sleep."

We have tried to establish now the nature of science. We have tried to examine it in terms of origin, identity and loss. We have tried to say what science is and to what degree it can legitimately lay claim to truth, while also suggesting that when science exceeds any claim other than the ability to study and articulate those dimensions of human existence in which we are all identical to the extent that this genuine identity can be resolved into the abstract, impersonal domain of mathematics, *its claim is false.*

Therefore, the claim of social science to any special preeminence in adoption is also false, precisely because adoption is an individual, personal, intimate, human reality involving all the elements and modalities of our being, touching on matters of the deepest heart and soul.

To the precise degree that every adoption is alike in a quantifiable, mathematically expressible way, social sciences is the preferred instrument for grasping its essential structure. But the measurable dimensions of the adoption experience, as is the case with any human experience, are not constitutive of its basic, fundamental reality, which in each circumstance is qualitatively distinct.

It should be said that all adoptive experiences *may* be alike on a spiritual, metaphysical level, but only in the sense that all experiences would qualitatively resemble each other rather than the identity persisting along a *quantifiable* continuum, which could be investigated by the methodology of modern science.

It would be rather the formal imagination, that is, the imagination of forms which works *analogically*, that would be the appropriate "instrument."

Why then does social science continue in its special status? In a moment, we shall explore this in greater depth, but here let me expose one of the intellectual ploys used by social science to maintain its status. The ploy is simply to dismiss all rival, alternative modes of research as "anecdotal" or "analogical" or personal, poetic, rhetorical, etc. The reason I call it a ploy rather than merely linking it with the usual "scientific imperialism" that tries to discredit all modes of knowledge and speech by dismissing them as "unscientific" is that at least the mathematical language of hard science is precise because physical realities and laws can be expressed by the precision of mathematics. *But human realities cannot.* Because the adoption experience is a human experience that can never be reduced to a formula, one will never be able to study adoption by opening a book that explains its essence in terms of mathematical formulas. There will never be something like Adoption = MC^2.

Hence, no grounds exist for attacking personal and poetic modes of articulating the basic psychological and spiritual structures of adoption because that is all that we will ever have. Further, no need exists to apologize for the empirical, phenomenological, inductive, even personal and intuitive aspects of social science research. If one were to take a social science text and deduct everything that will not qualify as "hard science," nothing would remain. So why not then simply dispense with the pretension of science and begin to speak personally, philosophically, spiritually, anecdotally and do so without the need to qualify?

What adoption needs is a touch of Blake.

*

Spotlight on Research

"Psychologists are now researching how the experience of being adopted in infancy affects the already complicated life of a teenager. Comparatively little is known currently about adopted teenagers and adoptive families in general.

"Are adopted teenagers more at risk than their non-adopted peers? How and what factors could minimize that risk, if so? These questions are the focal point of the largest-ever national study examining the needs of adopted teenagers and their families. Known as Service and Mental Health Needs of Adopted Adolescents (Adoptive Families), the study is being conducted by the Search Institute, a 34-year-old nonprofit research organization devoted to the study of children and adolescents. The Institute is located in Minneapolis, Minnesota.

"Funded by a $1-million grant from the National Institute of Mental Health, the project is now beginning the third of its three and a half year duration. It is in the process of contacting 1,700 families, with an ultimate goal of obtaining 1,000 families. This pool could involve up to 3,500 individual subjects.

"Formal data collection begins this month as the study enters its second phase. In the first phase, begun in July 1990, 600 open-ended questionnaires were sent to adopted teenagers and their adoptive parents. Researchers used the empirical data as the basis for writing items for the final data collection. These items were field-tested in fall 1991 on 150 youths and 230 adoptive parents."

"Teen Adopted in Infancy: Risk and Families"
in APS Observer Vol. 5, No. 2

Where adoption is concerned, the main instrument of social science research has been the questionnaire.

Social scientists themselves would have us believe that social science begins with the questionnaire. But social science begins where all sciences begin: with science; that is to say, with a conceptual infrastructure, a mental set of premises, a metaphysics about the nature of world, body, and in the case of the questionnaire, language.

The scientific world view reduces language to a quantifiable continuum of sameness. Emptied of their weight and wonder, their ecstasy and bulk, words become mere counters with little to distinguish between them and numbers, so that every statement about a similar topic, or every answer to a single question, may be viewed as having validity and identical value, and thus are strictly comparable.

But language cannot be so reduced. Words are not neutral counters that correspond to the qualitative reality of experience in a manner akin to how mathematics corresponds to nature's quantifiable dimensions. True words do not "correspond" to facts (truth as correspondence theory); instead, true words *reveal* meanings (truth as revelation). The "truest" language is the most *revealing* language in which we reveal both the nature of the subject under investigation and our own participation in that nature. Hence, in social science research, no two answers, no two protocols, can ever be counted strictly comparable.

Further every question (as any good trial attorney knows, but apparently social scientists do not know) predisposes. By virtue of both its metaphysical and phenomenological structure, every question is a leading question and every answer follows that lead. Not even all personal prejudices, biases and assumptions can be eschewed, much less the assumptions consubstantial with the scientific attitude.

Social science research employing questionnaires can never transcend its status as an ongoing conversation between one or a team of researchers and multiple subjects each of whose statements are qualitatively unique. The value of this conversation, therefore, also cannot be said to transcend its structure as a particular co-created human language event expressive of the interplay of intentions, motivation, interpretation, history, presence and the elusive, recalcitrant nature of the language medium itself. Just as through the efforts of its participants, any good conversation can distill the truth, so too can a conversation carried on under the rubric of social science research. But it does so, not "scientifically," but through the sophistication and deepening of insight that sometimes occurs amid the supple clarities, humorous evasions, and ecstatic lifts that occur in conversations between talented, gifted, well stocked minds. Social science as science can no more make a special claim on truth than the outcome of any human dialogue.

That's all we have. But it's not our pity. It's our glory. Our pity is that we forget.

*

"Positivist sociology tended to turn all of history into a closed system. Although critics have focused on the distant influence of Aristotle or the authority of organic metaphors in the romantic and Darwinian nineteenth century, the underlying premise for the practice of treating "society" or "history" as a unitary organism was the belief in deterministic natural laws. Just as the "economy" had tended to become a closed system of variables from whose action all change in the system could be deduced, so too did society."

Dorothy Ross, The Origins of American Social Science,
Cambridge University Press, 1991, p. 18

"Man is essentially social."

George Herbert Mead

". . . The Kingdom of God is within you."

Luke 17: 21

In the previous sections, I have questioned the monopoly of and, indeed, to some extent, the validity of the scientific approach to adoption. But what about the "social" in "social science?"

To my mind another main difficulty of social science is that it *over privileges* the social dimension of human experience. To which, "But that is what social science does. What do you expect it to do?" is a quite reasonable response, for that is the definition of social science, particularly sociology: to study reality as if it were socially constructed.

Fine, so long as the *"as if"* is not forgotten, or, in other words, fine, so long as *sociology recalls that reality is more than social* (which I'm not so sure it does) and so long as in any single field sociology, with its companion discipline, social work, is not allowed to dominate. But of course, sociology and social work do dominate adoption.

Reality is more than social. It is also spiritual, psychological, biological, genetic, and, above all, individual. Each of these perspectives might yield a different point of view on adoption from the one that currently prevails.

To consider one only: the archetypal point of view, which one finds in various forms of anthropology, poetry, psychology and literary criticism. In this mode of thought, archetypal is a word employed to describe any phenomena that appears to be universal, ubiquitous, and timeless. Although forms of "adoption kinship" do differ in different cultures and times, I think the evidence compels us to say that something "like" adoption, that is to say, something "like" a collective institution for caring for children to whom a parent does not have a biological tie is universal. (See for example John Boswell's <u>The Kindness of Strangers</u>.)

The archetypal point of view further assumes archetypes to be situated in human nature, in the human soul, so that the "understanding" of adoption would require that we assume adoption to be "essential," that is, an "archetypal" expression of some basic truth about human nature.

A more romantic-spiritual point of view might divine in adoption a revelation of a mystery of the human heart rather than a social solution to a threefold social problem.

Were alternative approaches more consistently and eloquently represented in adoption, the experience of adoption might change given that to some degree our experience is conditioned, if not wholly determined, by our ideas, or better said, the ideas available to us for insighting and articulating the meaning of our experience.

For example: Often I have heard adoptees describe themselves as having two mothers – a birthmother from whom they drew life and an adoptive mother who nurtured and parented them. What might be noted in this *dual mother* idea is the equal privileging of biological and social reality. Are they really equally important, and if so, in what sense?

Closed adoption offers a ready answer which is that the social reality is absolutely constitutive of identity. Worth remarking in this context is the compatibility of such a practice with any theory that insists that human reality is primarily and even essentially socially determined. Worth remarking, as well, is that both closed adoption and social role theory, which is the intellectual foundation of sociology, are both largely American and twentieth century phenomena. In remarking on this, I do not necessarily assert a causal relationship because I do not believe that the origin of closed adoption can be explained exclusively in terms of social variables; rather, I hold that closed adoption may be explained by certain universal, psychological processes whose translation into an institution requires the presence of certain operative sociological variables only one of which was the available rationalization provided by social role theory.

A more human, illuminating and therapeutic answer would begin with a phenomenology of adoption which in turn would be rooted in a philosophy more attuned and respectful of the diverse modalities of human existence – biological, psychological, spiritual, etc. In addition, this philosophy of humanity or "philosophy of man," to use the traditional term, or "phenomenological anthropology," to use the new one, must be grounded in a metaphysics not unwilling to answer fundamental questions about, *"What is humanity?"* and "What is its place and destiny in the cosmos?"

In the absence of such a philosophic context, it seems fairly easy to predict the demise of closed adoption even as social role theory is also on the decline. Spiritual questions and realities are increasingly emerging as a concern both in academic circles and the public debate. Social role theory is already itself under attack in the field of adoption by theorists more inclined to privilege biological and genetic factors in identity. Hence, the emphasis is now on the in-utero, birth and the pre-verbal experience of the infant.

We simply cannot answer questions about, *"Who is real?"* and *"What is real?"* and what ought to be legally mandated as reality, without first asking and answering, *"What is reality itself?"* We have to enter with philosophy into the realm of "ultimate concern."

To sum up now: I have questioned the preeminent status of the social sciences in adoption work on two grounds: first, its identification with a particular conceptual model, that of science, which by virtue of its own conceptual infrastructure is simply incapable of grasping the essential, human, intimate, emotional reality of adoption. Although the social sciences can make important contributions to the field, in no way do they merit any special preeminence. Second, I have pointed out the over privileging of social reality, or the *mitwelt* in phenomenological terms, to the exclusion of other elements of human experience that are more constitutive of our humanity *qua* humanity. I have also linked the rise of the social sciences in America with the emergence and entrenchment of the practice of closed adoption inasmuch as the fundamental premise of both sociology and closed adoption is that humanity is essentially and even exclusively a social creature, that is to say, human reality is socially constructed.

Now emerges the question of what accounts for this unmerited preeminence. Why does everyone in adoption ceaselessly prattle on about what research shows? Even if we succeeded in a persuasive, historical, archeology of the genesis of this condition, we must still account for its continuation. Why does it persist when there is no compelling justification for it?

*

"Philosophy, beginning in wonder, as Plato and Aristotle said, is able to fancy everything different from what it is. It sees the familiar as if it were strange, and the strange as if it were familiar. It can take things up and lay them down again. Its mind is full of air that plays round every subject. It rouses us from our native dogmatic slumber and breaks up our caked prejudices. Historically it has always been a sort of fecundation of four different human interests, science, poetry, religion, and logic, by one another. It has sought by hard reasoning for results emotionally valuable. To have some contact with it, to catch its influence, is thus good for both literary and scientific students. By its poetry it appeals to literary minds; but its logic stiffens them up and remedies their softness. By its logic it appeals to the scientific; but softens them by its other aspects, and saves them from too dry a technicality. Both types of student ought to get from philosophy a livelier spirit, more air, more mental background. 'Hast any philosophy in thee, Shepherd?' – this questions of Touchstone's is the one with which men should always meet one another. A man with no philosophy in him is the most inauspicious and unprofitable of all possible social mates."

William James, The Writings of William James, p. 475

In the poetry of William Blake, the new scientific attitude, which was just then emerging into the prominence that it still enjoys today, is personified in the guise of Urizen who yearns to impose upon the world, as Blake describes it:

> *"One command, one joy, one desire,*
> *One curse, one weight, one measure,*
> *One King, one God, one Law,"*

despite the fact, as Blake says elsewhere in one of his aphorisms, where he intends to distinguish between the world of quality-wisdom and quantity-science, "One Law for the Lion and Ox is Oppression."

Urizen materializes as a restless, agitated creature, loaded down with the heavy books of observation that he always carries with him, and always engaged in the great adventure of scientific discovery. But in Blake, Urizen never rests; he is condemned to infinite research, because the ultimate wisdom that he seeks can never be attained through scientific method. The wisdom that he seeks is qualitative in nature and corresponds to reality considered in its qualitative and essential human being. Although scientific methodology grasps truth, it is not *the Truth* in which the soul can rest, lying down in green pastures beside the still waters. Such truth corresponds only to the true imagination. Hence, Urizen can never sleep, never rest; he just works on and on "down falling thro' immensity for ever and ever."

Blake understood that the chemical analysis of grapes will never yield the warm, dark, earthy, wooden, sultry taste of the juices of the vine.

Blake might have inscribed on Urizen's tombstone, "All the data is still not in."

So with social science in adoption. Social science research can never elaborate a fundamental truth about adoption. It can never tell us what adoption is or how to allay or abolish the suffering involved. By its very nature, social science is disqualified from such a task.

And yet, we in the adoption field, that is, we who are engaged in the actual practice of adoption, act as if our practice were somehow supported by the "research" and the conclusions drawn therefrom. And to the extent that we know and acknowledge our limitations and errors we act as if a further advance in knowledge and correction of those errors were just a matter of time, more data, more research, which is always being carried on – well, someone is doing it, somewhere, in the sociology and social work departments of the university. And we are very glad to participate in and support such research whenever possible.

But of course, this is a complete delusion in that no research existing anywhere has ever, does now or ever will furnish sufficient data or results to scientifically legitimize professional adoption practice.

But by pretending that it does or might or will in some distant point in the future when all the data is in and has been exhaustively analyzed, sociology and social work departments are maintained in business and often awash on federal money, while practicing professionals avoid the risk and challenge and *radical uncertainty* of philosophy, the ascent of mind; we avoid the need to think critically and rigorously about our work and its philosophical and spiritual implications. As Ortega says: "Philosophy, then, is not a science but, if you like, an indecency, since it consists in baring things and oneself, stripping them to stark nakedness – to what they are and I am – and that is all." Further, we are able to avoid genuine, sophisticated philosophical scrutiny of our profession. In short, by colluding with social science, we keep from having to work too hard or think too much or read too much, but most of all we avoid facing the fact that adoption practice inevitably involves and raises the most basic, fundamental questions about what it means to be human, which means that those who practice in the field and wish to practice ethically and compassionately must themselves in their heart of hearts, their soul of souls, give an answer to those questions. Because adoption does raise perennial, timeless philosophical and spiritual questions, because adoption involves matters of what Tillich called, "ultimate concern," to practice adoption requires an ongoing *auseinandersetzung* or confrontation with one's own most secret innermost spiritual self. To practice adoption ethically requires that we look through the glass darkly and confront the abyss of ourselves. And as Nietzsche said, "He who looks too long in the abyss, finds the abyss is looking back at him." Adoption work itself, then, becomes a spiritual journey, a means of polishing the heart.

To accept the burden of philosophy, to read, to think, to study till we drop, to confront our own frailties and falsehoods, our own shadows and abyss, would endow the worker, the person who has so dipped into the oblivion of his own heart and suffered the spiritual crisis that results from this nekyia, with *authority.*

What is authority? Who has it?

To paraphrase Norman O. Brown in his "Apocalypse of the Mind," I come to you not as one with authority but as one who has some idea of where to look for it.

Authority is what the centurion in Matthew 7:8-13 recognized in the Christ who can merely say a word and the servant will be healed.

It is the authority Blake lays claim to when he says, "Hear the voice of the Bard / Who present, past and future sees."

Though not coercive, authority does compel. By others a person who has authority is felt to body forth the truth. It is as if he has an aura, a presence that both compels and reassures. Those around him feel both safe while also moved, inspired and challenged. A charismatic, caring person with authority, need merely walk into a room and begin to speak about the theme, the subject in which he has authority and others are instantly alert and conscious of the fact that here is "someone who knows what he's talking about," who, in the old language, "knows whereof they speak." Rather than status or position, a person with authority may be said to have human stature and charismatic presence.

Since authority is unequivocally an individual reality, that is, only individuals have authority, not institutions, the expression of authority can only occur through modes of presence and language that are equally intimate and individual. One can't expect to have authority without being willing to be tested, without being willing to stand before a crowd in order for them to see what you are made of. Before they assumed the purple, the Roman emperors were required to display themselves before the troops, so that the troops might take their individual measure. For language to convey authority, it must ebb and flow, pulse and flame with the speaker's individual reality. His breath must wing his words; his rhythm time them. Impersonal, neutral, scientific prose is entirely unsuited as a medium for expression of authority, whereas art, poetry and rhetoric serve as an ideal medium.

After reading articles in a sociology journal, no reader raises his head and says, "I must change my life," which is exactly what Rilke did after viewing a statue of Apollo and what millions of Americans once did after hearing John Kennedy, Robert Kennedy or Martin Luther King. It is what they have been doing in the Eastern Block Countries over the last year. Each of these three Americans as well as Havel and Yeltsin and others have the authority of which Christ and the great romantics spoke. It comes from within. A dazzle of very human truth.

Authority grows with experience. So authority in adoption would begin either with the experience of adoption as a birthparent or, adoptive parent or an adoptee or in the experience of adoption work. The experience must then be challenged and critiqued by philosophical interrogation and scrutiny, then distilled by spiritual concerns and practice until becoming a quintessence of pure vision, a pure vision that then returns to illuminate the original experience from within. This process, however, does not unfold in linear succession. *We are not talking about training here; we are talking about transformation.* All these illuminations occur simultaneously, so that even as we work, we study and even as we study, we open up our hearts.

Where there is both a need and desire to educate, but authority is lacking, power soon fills the void. One of the most extraordinary aspects of social work is the power that the discipline wields on both an institutional and a personal level. For someone whose entry into the adoption field came through philosophy and psychology rather than through sociology and social work, the power present truly is astonishing. Under normal circumstances when such power is wielded, it is done so only within a context of multiple checks and controls. This is simply not so in adoption social work.

Indeed, as David Kirk has said, "the claims of competence staked by social work in adoption tended to be spurious." (Kirk, Adoptive Kinship, p. 94.)

Power corrupts and absolute power corrupts absolutely, so runs the old truism. Over the last century, adoption work has become corrupt in all too many cases. Unfortunately, the corruption is not flamboyant or excessive in ways that would make it easily identifiable. Rather it is the more pernicious form of laziness, inertia, institutional smugness, mediocrity, poor and undemanding preparation of the professional, hypocrisy and complacency, and widespread polite collusion in platitudes and cliches. It is the corruption of the *luke-warm*, of what Christ called, "the Pharisees and Sadducees," that is, the legalistic, conformist element in every soul that opposes the spirit of the Prophets. It is the corruption that weeps with sentimentality but remains dry-eyed when the suffering is real.

In all the Great Romantics, the true enemy, the true corruption always lies within and is present within every human soul. Sometimes it appears in hypocrisy, sometimes it appears in ideological purity and arrogance. Shelley called it the "unwilling dross that checks the spirit's flight." It is not the big lies that we tell ourselves but the little ones that finally corrupt and do us in. We do go out with a whimper and not with a bang.

Coleridge symbolized this inner constriction as the white albatross that the Ancient Mariner is forced to wear around his neck. As it has crystallized in adoption, that albatross is simply the illusion that the scientific method will ever set us free; ever set adoptees, adoptive parents and birthparents free from the sorrow and pain of adoption so that they in unison might find the blessed balm of love and hope. Science cannot. It has not. It never will. We must look elsewhere. With fear and trembling, with the torch of true philosophy held high above our heads and the golden bough of spiritual tradition going on before us, we must go down into the dark place of the heart. The dusk and dawn are there, so too, a human face.

Every Night and every Morn
Some to Misery are Born.
Every Morn and every Night
Some are Born to Sweet Delight.
Some are Born to Sweet Delight,
Some are Born to Endless Night.
We are led to Believe a Lie
When we see not Thro' the Eye,
Which was Born in a Night to perish in a Night,
When the Soul Slept in Beams of Light.
God Appears, and God is Light,
To those poor souls who dwell in Night;
But does a Human Form Display
To those who Dwell in Realms of Day.

—*William Blake*
"Auguries of Innocence"

*

Adoption Politics

Adoptee Voices

Back this week from another adoption conference. This one took place in Austin, Texas where it was sponsored by Adoption Knowledge Affiliates, a diverse, exciting, spirited group committed to ethical adoption practice and legislation.

As is so often the case at conferences where adult adoptees are present, together with birth and adoptive parents, I returned a little ashamed of myself and of everyone else who has been involved in institutional adoption for the last forty years.

I say forty years, because it was not until the decade following the end of World War II that as a society we began to experiment with adoption practices that not only severed all ties between adoptees and their natural families of origin but concealed the very identities of those families by sealing the records of birth and substituting new "birth" certificates that bore the names of the adoptive parents.

No one can fault the motives of those who created this system. Like most of the social planners and social engineers who have walked through this century, their motives, at least, at the start, were essentially noble although alloyed, perhaps, with a touch of arrogance. They believed that with sufficient education and with the proper environment human nature could be remade, refashioned according to a better plan, a higher or more developed type. Social planners everywhere believed that once humankind could be liberated from the burdens of the past and freed of the limitations that history and biology seem to impose upon our natures, we all could reach a new peak of happiness and fulfillment. By sweeping away all the old traditions, whatever be their form in the way that a developer might clear away an old neighborhood in order to make way for more modern buildings, social engineering would accomplish this. In adoption this meant the closed adoption system. Nurture would not only cooperate and support nature and reform it where possible and necessary, nurture would *remake* nature by abolishing it altogether. Biology, genetics, history, culture, tradition, parent and kin – even the event of birth itself – could all be erased.

At the end of this century, we know that social engineering has failed. When men and women forfeit their history, culture and kin, they suffer. They become shadows of all they might have been, although to others they may seem fine or even remarkable success stories. A fresh start, a thousand new and otherwise impossible opportunities, generous love and nurture do not eliminate this loss. It grieves the heart even as that heart may leap with love and gratitude for these new blessings. History is in us – it pulses in our heart. Genetics plays through our lives in ways so subtle as to be impossible to map. We are our parents' children, then, the ones from whom we drew breath and life, so that our nature will always reflect the color of their eyes, the flash of their smile and the stride of their walk, so that we will always echo them in the rhythm of our heart and even in the patterns of our brains. Nothing can erase or alter this, although our characters will also bear the imprints that many others make, especially adults, who love and cherish us, and, perhaps, share their hearts and homes in the role of mentor, teacher, fosterer or adoptive parents. But if we are such stuff as dreams are made of, we're also flesh and bone.

Biology may be overbilled in parenting but it is not overbilled in life. Indeed, the need for parenting depends upon the intimate, mysterious, very physical acts of conception, pregnancy and birth. The connection is inescapable. To deny this connection is to deny the conditions of our humanity, which means that any policy built upon this denial, no matter how subtlety constructed, vigorously argued, or powerfully entrenched, or even compassionately intended, will ultimately be inhumane.

We also know that to deny the past and to renounce tradition is not without often tragic consequences. Which returns me to my experience at the conference and my shame at the way that adoptees have been exploited in this century as virtual human experiments not unlike, in some ways, other victims of other massive attempts to *"recreate"* humanity (always in a noble cause, of course.)

To attend these conferences is to be overwhelmed by the grief, loss, anger and frustration of adult men and women, adult adoptees who not only, without their consent, and through no fault of their own, were deprived at birth of the comfort and self-knowledge that comes to the rest of us through connection to our history and kin, but continue to be denied what would seem the inalienable right to simply know the names of the men and women who gave them life and to have the chance to look into their eyes and be told the story. That every adoptee does not feel this way is not relevant. That one should is enough to condemn our present system. But of course, many adoptees do feel this way. Each year, braving the risk of misunderstanding or rejection, thousands of adoptees search for their birthparents. And for every adoptee who does search there are a dozen more whose hearts turn over with questions to which they never give voice for fear of hurting their parents.

Knowing as we do that in almost every other field of human existence that social engineering has failed, how can we continue to defend it in adoption? How can we continue closed adoption? The past is important, history resurfaces – in politics, in the city, in religion, in poetry, in the heart. How can we continue to keep birth and adoption records sealed?

But most critically, how, whether it be on the editorial pages of major papers or in the halls of the state legislature or at the board meetings of adoption agencies, can we continue to let adoptive parents, or birthparents, or professionals, or community leaders, speak and decide for adoptees? In each of these centers of influence and power, adoptees (and birthparents) are sparsely represented, while adoptive parents are over represented. Time and time again, during the course of my career, I have seen powerful adoptive parents who, confusing their own needs with the need of their child, kill a story, an article, or piece of legislation whose only purpose was to bring their son or daughter what they themselves had spent a lifetime striving to provide: self-understanding, self-acceptance, self-worth. To paraphrase Shakespeare once again, *"Hath not an adoptee eyes, flesh and voice and a heart that yearns and aches not to undo the past but to know it and to embrace it, if it be his or her will?"* Until adoptees' voices are heard and their point of view institutionally and by law represented, illegitimacy describes not the condition of a birth, but the morality of our collective decisions about adoption.

When I am asked if I am pro-adoption, if that nomenclature intends to describe a position of advocacy for adoptees, defending their right to have every chance in life, including the chance to know and embrace their origins, my answer is *"Yes."*

But if by pro-adoption, it is meant support of an act of social engineering that transfers a child from one family to another and then forbids all memory, contact and knowledge of the original family, my answer is *No.*

And if pro-adoption means decisions made *"in the best interest of the child,"* which truly is a blank slate on which adults are free to project their competing interests, my answer is also *"No."*

There are some responsibilities in life that cannot be signed away. There are some rights which cannot be acquired through a signature. Birth and historical connections cannot be signed away. The right to deny those connections cannot be acquired.

To be pro-adoption means to be pro-adoptee – ADOPTEE, not "adopted child." To be pro-adoption means to be respectful and supportive of adoptees who, in the depths of their personhood, must in the present know and come to terms with their past so that they may freely determine their future.

Adoptees are not blank slates, not at birth, not ever. They have beating hearts and eyes that moisten and voices that crack with emotion, and fears that haunt them, and memories that grieve for what's lost, and arms that reach out for understanding and love, from the parents who raised and love them, from the parents who gave them life, from us all.

Constrained by our own insecurities, must we continue to turn away?

*

Liberals & Conservatives

Meditating all these things tonight together with the current state of adoption politics as I drive along a back country road. It really is a beautiful evening: a golden Texas autumnal dusk, the air brushed clean and sparkling, white cattle nearby on a green hillside knee deep in evening shadow.

That sweeping this country is a massive reaction against serious adoption reform, which would do anything other than prop up the present system, largely by limiting birthparent rights, is hardly in doubt.

The indictment, conviction and now imminent jailing of Sandy Musser, a search consultant, who aids adoptees who wish to contact their natal parents, as a result of a government "sting"; the venomous *New Yorker* article on the Deboer case which was foreshadowed by an earlier "expose" of open adoption; the publication of Elizabeth Bartholet's (a Harvard law professor) *Family Bonds: Adoption and the Politics of Parenting*, which was puffed in a *Times* book review that singles out for special praise her chapter debunking the "adoption stigma"; the sudden resurgence of the National Committee of Adoption, which has even undergone a name change to the National Council for Adoption, a political lobby whose spokesmen often pose as Child Welfare experts. These particulars top a very crowded list.

(A word about the National Council: they've been especially active as of late. Eager to exploit the tragedy of the Deboers, they have recently disseminated nationwide to adoptive parent groups free copies of Lucinda Frank's New Yorker piece, which was followed by a personal letter from William Pierce, with invitation to join the council and exchange newsletters and information.)

Since the *New Yorker* and the *New York Times* generally speak from the philosophical and political left, one might expect in matters of adoption reform to find a few conservative voices in lonely, dissent. But one looks in vain for a challenge.

National Review ran a cover story in which the author caricatured the very idea of adoption reform, while trying to link adoption reform with abortion. At *First Things*, John Neuhaus regularly promotes the National Committee as a reliable authority on ethical adoption. In a *First Things* review, Ms. Bartholet's book welcomed high praise. Conservative politicians are now touting active, high profile, pro-adoption policies as a credible alternative to abortion.

The absence of a conservative challenge surprises – indeed, dismays – because if there is anything essential to conservative philosophy as it has developed in this century, it is spirited, eloquent resistance to the sort of social engineering that closed adoption represents. From Ortega to Voegelin, to Kendall to Buckley, Burke to Kirk, the position is the same: social engineering strikes at the heart of who we are as human beings and always bears the sign of that most ancient heresy: *gnosis.* And when did conservatives ever accept social workers and social "scientists," Harvard attorneys, or Washington lobbies as reliable guides in matters of the human heart? Many will remember the famous story of Frank Meyer who when the social worker came to his door to explain that he needed permission to home school his kids shouted defiantly from the next room: *"You need **my** permission to do anything with my children, I don't need **yours**."*

How uncommonly strange it is, then, to see conservative journals of opinion, such as *National Review* or *First Things* embrace the obviously "modernist" idea of closed adoption. When did conservatives forsake their tolerance and sympathy, their admiration for rooted, traditional hearth and kin in order to celebrate the barbecue pit and the American two parent nuclear, suburban, consumer family, cut off from the past, and often contemptuous of all inherited things as the cure for all evil? To use a Faulknerian metaphor, it is as if we're all Snopses now. When did conservatives embrace the Lockean idea of the tabula rasa and human nature as re-creatable at will?

The answer is that conservatives have never made these choices. What conservatives have done is grasp for almost any alternative to the exponentially rising number of abortions or have responded sympathetically to friends and family desperate to raise a family of their own but unable to conceive. Or without ever inquiring too closely into the conditions under which a child might have come into a home, that is, without ever scrutinizing what passes for standard adoption practice, they identify with adoptive parents in their agony as they are forced by the courts to return a child to birthparents who have changed their mind about relinquishment. But social engineering has never been the solution for any evil or human tragedy, except in the most superficial manner. With closed adoption, the situation is no different.

The irony about what ought to be the conservative view of closed adoption is that it has been mostly people with conservative sympathies who run adoption. *"Where is the power?"* Willmore Kendall, a major conservative theorist, used to insist is the fundamental political question. In adoption, the answer remains: on the boards of traditional agencies, which are often church affiliated and whose members tend to be prominent business leaders with generally conservative political views. Thus at the heart of the adoption system, where decisions are made and power exercised, we find people supporting policies in sharp conflict with their philosophy as expressed in most other situations. At the heart of the adoption has existed the incredible contradiction of *"conservatives"* using social engineering to enforce *"conservative"* family values. A generation ago David Kirk noted that adoption was being used to prop up the modern nuclear family at a time when it appeared to be disintegrating. What I add to his analysis is the self-contradiction involved in conservative agency boards using social engineering to achieve this. All the coercive sentimentality that continues to engulf the adoption process, robbing it of what ought to be its solemnity and gravity, may well be an unconscious *"arrangement"* (in Adler's sense) intended to conceal this contradiction.

When one finds left and right joining arms, one of two things is occurring: the millennium, or convergence of personal self-interest masquerading as philosophical amity. I think the second is the case, which has always been so in adoption. Since no one, with the requisite training, has ever seriously philosophically examined adoption, self-interest has governed. Adoptive parents, whose philosophical or political contentions were otherwise legion, could nonetheless sit on boards or in editor's chairs, sip coffee, make small talk and agree to keep records and adoptions closed. If social workers colluded with them – that was all the better, and powerful, high profile people would suddenly defer to the *"professional advice"* of people whose opinions they cared next to nothing about in any other respect.

Over the last ten years, adoption reformers have been challenging this collusion. And not without some success, which explains perhaps both the intensity of the current anti-reform reaction and the fact that instead of simply playing a more savvy political game and quoting ambiguous studies, which it often had a part in funding, the anti-reform movement has gone in search of an intellectually respectable foundation. In other words, the anti-reformers have been looking for a book to quote, preferably by someone from Harvard. It appears to have found one in Elizabeth Bartholet's *Family Bonds: Adoption and the Politics of Parenting.*

*

Brave New Nurture

Family Bonds puts me in mind of William F. Buckley's famous witticism about how he'd rather be governed by the first hundred names in the Boston telephone book than by the Harvard faculty. After completing this book, I would add to Mr. Buckley's remark that I would much rather adoption be governed by forty first year adoption workers than by this Harvard professor.

Why? Is not this overwhelmingly harsh? I don't think so, because the average first year adoption worker usually has not forgotten her (or his) humanity – the humanity that knows that sexuality and the body are essential dimensions of our being. Our bodies give us joy and rapture, but also death and tragedy. And these first year workers know that to bring a child into this world, to carry it through pregnancy, and to give birth, the miracle of birth, and then to give that child away would have to be something whose aftershock and lingering effect would be tremendous, would have to scar the spirit even if the most fundamental wounding in time could heal. These first year workers have not forgotten the normal human dream of marrying, of having and raising a child together, a child in whose looks, smiles, gestures and aspirations, one finds reflected not only one's own traits and character but also traits and character of those whom one loves and remembers as being a part of one's life. In all likelihood, they are experiencing this dream themselves. And, finally, they have not forgotten the very human joy in being around one's own kind, one's own kin, with whom one feels not only instantly connected but also through them connected to generations past. They have not forgotten the comfort and reassurance of looking into the mirror as an anxious teenager and seeing the features of someone they know and love and admire looking back.

This humanity that enables one to intimately and instantly empathize with the loss and grief that are part of the story of every adoption is precisely what makes a good worker, someone to whom birthparent, adoptive parent and adoptee can all look for support.

This humanity is what is missing from *Family Bonds*, especially from the chapter *"Adoption and Stigma."* In the first few paragraphs of this chapter, Ms. Bartholet manages to dismiss, or at least, minimize, all of these experiences, which makes her view, in the very strictest sense, inhumane.

The argument in this chapter is very clever in that the author realizes quite clearly that an adoption system based on social engineering is inevitably philosophically flawed and practically unjust, but she then flips reality on its head to argue that the very human grief, loss and pain that birthparents and infertile couples might feel, the unity that every mother and father instantly feel with the child to whom they give life, the desire of an adoptee to know and connect to the natal parents and to the traditions, culture, observances, and the generations to which they connect and embody is the result of conditioning. Birthparents, infertile couples and society as a whole are *"conditioned"* to feel this way by *"those in charge of regulating adoption* or *the regulatory structure that reinforces the stigma."*

In order to establish just how widespread this *"conditioning"* is, Ms. Barthelot then proceeds, within the space of a few paragraphs, to dismiss the wisdom of fairy tales, classical mythology, the Old Testament, Western literature, ordinary popular wisdom, and the cruel but innocent *"out of the mouths of babes"* kind of truth that is blurted out daily on every blacktop and next to every water fountain in every elementary school in this country.

One begins to wonder what is left from which to draw truth and insight about the adoption experience if we're going to dismiss just about everything that constitutes our philosophical and literary heritage? After you rule out everyone from Sophocles, to the Brothers Grimm to the author of Bible, who's left?

To be honest, what and who is left, are a few social science studies, several of which were done by an apparent friend who wrote a blurb for the back cover.

I mean, really, come on. What actually characterizes these texts, as well as the works of the reformers, is a complex, sympathetic vision of the existential, human meaning of adoption. In her discussion of the *"adoption stigma,"* Ms. Bartholet performs the amazing feat of misreading sympathy as stigma, and a respect for human rights and human dignity as a desire to control.

The fact is that the adoption *"stigma"* as the author cleverly denominates it, is in fact part of the phenomenology of every adoption. And the true social conditioning that has plagued the adoption system throughout this century, and which this book cleverly reinforces, has always been in the service of denying the truth, which is not an *"ugly"* or *"horrible"* truth but the very human truth that one cannot separate a child from his mother, his parents, his culture, his race, his memories, all of his ancestral voices and ancestral heritage without this separation causing pain, grief, loss and, should the reality of this loss be denied throughout his life, devastating problems. Further, the *"stigmatizers,"* such as Baran and Pannor, or B.J. Lifton, whose positions she viciously parodies, and those very few agencies where open adoption and open records receive authentic support, are not in control of either the institution of adoption itself or even of what most professionals believe about adoption. In sharp contrast to the picture presented here Baran, Pannor, B.J. Lifton as well as a dozen other reformers who might be named are mavericks and even heroes who have been willing to speak and defend the truth even in the face of immensely powerful opposition.

Truly, Ms. Bartholet is extremely cagey on this social engineering question. In fact, she concludes her book with a rousing call for *"deregulation"* of adoption. That's right *"deregulation."*

> "We need to deregulate adoption. The current regulatory framework creates obstacles on both a pragmatic and a psychological level: it makes the adoption process costly and unpleasant, and it simultaneously degrades and demeans this form of family. Indeed, it is clear that the essential point of the current framework is to maintain barriers to adoption so as to ensure that this form of family arrangement can be kept in its place as a last resort. We need, therefore, to deregulate in all the ways discussed in this book. We need

new policies that focus on the positive rather than the negative potential of adoption. For example, we need meaningful guarantees the children will receive nurturing homes and will not be held in limbo for longer than absolutely necessary. We need new systems providing financial reimbursement for some of the costs involved in adoption, so that more of those who are interested in this form of parenting are able to pursue it."

However, when we get down to particulars, especially if it involves adoptees or birthparents, *"deregulation"* goes by the wayside right quick. Here she is on open adoption.

"While greater openness seems the appropriate move for the future, the politics of adoption today make decisions about what steps to take now very complicated. In the current context, a move to embrace openness might further denigrate rather than affirm adoption. The pressure for openness is coming from a movement that is profoundly hostile to adoption as a family form. In addition, today's world is one in which we are all bombarded on a regular basis with messages that reinforce the significance of biologically linked parenting. In this world birth parents are something of a threat to the viability of adoptive families. In a future world in which the stigma surrounding adoption and infertility has been eliminated or at least significantly reduced, opening records should send a signal that birth family links are real and relevant but not of necessary and central importance to an adoptee's personhoood or to parenting relationships. The establishment of an open-record system today might send a very different signal."

Despite her use of very appealing terminology, inasmuch as it would seem to grasp the relevant philosophical issues, Ms. Bartholet tends to support *"deregulation,"* only when it would benefit adoptive parents, who in her argument come very close, it would appear, to having an absolute right to parent, while everyone else must wait until the golden age when human nature changes, or, more ominously, is changed, to better accord with the vision of social engineers.

Ironically, *"deregulation"* of the adoption system along lines proposed by the author would increase the likelihood of more Wars for Baby Jessica. What has received little play in the media is the reason the Deboer's chose not to adopt in their home state of Michigan. It is because the adoption system in Michigan is *"regulated"* (regulated in the way that street lights regulate traffic,) that is to say, an attempt has been made in Michigan to both represent the best interest of the child while also protecting both birth and adoptive parents' rights which can conflict. In Iowa, the law was very *"flexible,"* so flexible in fact, that the birthmother in this case received no counseling, the relinquishment was taken by a lawyer representing the Deboers, and, at least according to Mrs. Schmidt's description, the doctor and hospital staff applied what she felt to be some pressure. Basically, no one who knew anything about adoption, about the ambivalence and anguish that is attendant upon nearly every relinquishment, was in any way involved. If adoption is to be *unregulated* in this manner the only way to protect children from the trauma that Jessica underwent would be to severely limit birthparent rights, especially birthfather rights. Again, what that kind of deregulation proposed by Bartholet amounts to is turning over the whole institution to the control of adoptive parents.

But not just any adoptive parents. In a totally unregulated adoption system, it would be largely the brightest, most successful, most *empowered* adoptive parents, the ones who have friends who are doctors and lawyers or Harvard professors, who are connected to what is often euphemistically called *referral networks* who would always have the advantage. Less sophisticated, empowered people who hope to adopt would have a hard time of it, as many already do. Bartholet's vision of an adoption world where agencies would mainly be recruiters and *empowerers* of prospective adoptive parents is really not so far from the truth that is already in place as more and more adoption agencies recreate themselves in the image of *facilitators* who merely *assist* adoptive parents in *networking* in order to find birthparents who are then referred to the agency or directly arrange placement with the couple who *found* them. The prospective adoptive parents who for right or wrong reasons find this process uncomfortable are likely to wait for a long time, if not forever, for a child. The social work *matchers* who incur such opprobrium in this book have in reality almost vanished.

And yet, once again, we find that under the guise of *deregulation,* the author is in favor of restoring the old system, indeed the worst aspect of the old system, which was the obvious preference given by agencies to socio-economically successful white parents.

It's not deregulation, Ms. Bartholet is after, it's restoration of the traditional adoption system which was run largely at the pleasure of and for the sake of successful adoptive parents. The only features of the present adoption system that she is eager to dispense with are those that reflect genuine reform.

Also problematic is Ms. Bartholet's position on cross-racial placement. Put bluntly, she favors it and caricatures the position of those in opposition.

> "Racial matching policies represent a coming together of powerful and related ideologies – old-fashioned white racism, modern-day black nationalism, and what I will call 'biologism'..."

For me, she also shows a shade too much of the social engineer's delight in the trans-racial adoptive family as a model for social change.

> "From this perspective, which I share, transracial adoptive families constitute an interesting model of how we might better learn to live with one another in this society. These families can work only if their members have an appreciation of racial difference and a love that transcends such difference. And the evidence indicates that these families do work."

The problem with cross-racial adoption is not whether such families *work,* whatever that means. And, certainly, the issue is not whether love can cross racial lines and whether adults of a different race from their children make good parents. On the back porches, in the kitchens, in the nurseries, in the bottomless greenness of the deep Southern woods, African-Americans have been proving to whites for generation after generation that love, especially love of an adult for a child, and of a child for an adult, knows no color lines and will triumph over and transcend even the most viciously racist system. The problem with cross-racial adoptions today is that just not much of an effort has been made or is made in your average adoption agency or state system to genuinely serve the African- American community. Ms. Bartholet overestimates the difficulty in changing this situation and underestimates the subtle, but nonetheless effective prejudices and simple failure by professionals to think and work hard enough that explains the present situation and also explains why the difficulties black kids encounter growing up in white culture with white parents should not be minimized or denied just because they cannot be understood by social science studies and questionnaires.

In addition, given her enthusiasm for new family forms not based on or comparable to the two parent, biological family, the author ought to be more willing to at least consider the possibility that fostering and the foster care system might be reformed and renewed in such a way as at least to be less destructive on a child's psyche than currently is the case.

While my own position has moderated through the years, so that I no longer oppose cross-racial adoption on principle, I still can't help feeling a sense of injustice and regret when encountering arguments such as Ms. Bartholet's, which seem so willing not only to accept an injustice about the adoption system, but to benefit from it. If all restrictions limiting cross-racial placement are lifted tomorrow, it will be mostly white adoptive parents who benefit. Perhaps, many African-American children will benefit too, given their abandonment to the foster care system, where they often wait forever, with hearts shattered, hope lost, history destroyed. But I don't believe that one must be utopian or unrealistic to believe that with only a little additional effort on the part of the institution, more prospective African-American adoptive parents would respond. In fact, the evidence is strong that when genuine effort is made to reach out to the African-American community and when they find African-Americans in positions of authority in the adoption agency, they do respond in large numbers.

Clearly, we do need to do something. But it is a question of priorities. More African-Americans professionals in adoption; more effort made to recruit African-American adoptive parents; reform of the foster care system, *now*; and while this is occurring, fewer restrictions of cross racial placement. But to lift restrictions without simultaneously implementing these other three steps is both wrong and involves cross-racial placement advocates in a self-contradiction. If the first three steps are so impossible, does not this mean that the prejudice in our society truly is as great and as insurmountable as the most ideological Black separatist might maintain? And if so, are not cross-racial placements therefore themselves ill-advised?

Now, with all this said, let me make clear two points of agreement with Ms. Bartholet. First, I think the phenomenology of adoption does foreshadow, in a sometimes miraculous way, how we might overcome all the individual differences that divide us in order to enter into one common life, in order to belong to one extended family. For this reason, in many traditions, the ideal relationship existing between humanity and God is imaged as adoption.

Second, I agree that to limit the idea of family to blood kinship is a mistake. I would even call it an outrage. The far older, more universal meaning of family is *household* and there could be and usually were many members of one's household to whom there was no blood tie. One's family was not those to whom one felt bonded or attached, but to whom one felt close, with whom one shared the warmth of the fire, the trust of intimacy, the satisfaction of a meal, the challenge of work, the ordeal of hard times, the security of a routine, and, of course, the vital, vibrant, vital glow of love.

The irony is that it is just this definition of the family, which receives Ms. Bartholet's full support, to which adoption reform is trying to return us.

To oppose the social engineering American definition of adoption is not to oppose adoption. Adoption, fostering, mentoring, the family reaching out to take in their needy kin are familiar in all traditional cultures. Fostering was a common practice in Roman, Celtic, Arabic and ancient and medieval European culture. But the extension of love and support to children to whom one was not biologically connected never presumed to the fiction of creation of a totally new identity. One's kin folk were still one's kin folk even if they be unprepared, unwilling, or even undeserving of the rights and responsibilities of raising a child. To take in another person's child was understood to be a form of family preservation, a means by which a familiar community could enrich a child's experience, add to the delicate web of connections that surrounded and supported him, or even a means by which other understanding adults could compensate for human weakness and sin. "Whatever we do to the least of these" my grandmother might have said as she took in niece and nephew and a half dozen other kids at various times when times got hard or parents failed in their responsibilities.

Whether we call this guardianship or adoption is not the point. My grandmother would no more have discouraged some child from calling her mother, if that be the need of the child, than she would have refused to tuck him in bed at night or fix his supper. And if, for some legal protection or right, it was necessary to go to court, to *legalize* some living arrangement or connection, she would never have hesitated, knowing as she did that it is always love not the law that makes a parent real to a child. But she wouldn't have tried to pretend she was something she was not, nor would she have hushed a child from crying because he missed his mother or his dad, regardless of what she thought of them. And she would have expected them to cry.

Adoption will always be with us – thank goodness – because there will always be parents unable or unwilling to parent their children. There will always be real abandonment, abuse and neglect. There will always be hunger. And any time that it would truly benefit a child to be raised by others, thank goodness that there are others who in their generosity of spirit and love are willing to share their hearts and their homes. What's an adoptive family made of, if not genes and biology? Heart and soul can be the only answer. But not at the expense of the truth of our humanity, not at the expense of our *flesh*. Adoptive parenting is a high calling, a spiritual vocation, not a *solution* to a problem. To use the famous distinction of Gabriel Marcel, adoption belongs to the order of mystery rather than problems. Only a philosophical-spiritual viewpoint is capable of grasping its unique purpose and significance. We must take adoption out of the hands of the social engineers and the social planners, out of the hands of those who refuse to remember, as Unamuno said, that we are men and women of flesh and bones, out of the hands of those who refuse to remember the reality and significance of origins.

The key to a fair, true and compassionate adoption system is the idea of the person. Developed during the fifth century by Christian theologians and philosophers in an effort to explain the dual divine-human nature of Christ, in this century the idea has proved its richness and relevance to philosophical grasp of the essentials of the human condition. As a person, each of us is an individual who combines within our existence two natures – body and soul, matter and spirit, brain and consciousness, nature and nurture, etc. Neither element can be denied without diminishing our humanity.

For most of us, the dual nature of humanity can remain an interesting philosophical problem but for the adoptee it is the riddle of their being. They experience in a very direct way what most of us only philosophically consider. To become who they are, to become a person content in their personhood they must, through an act of personal insight and healing, rejoin body and soul, past and future, genetics and spirit in a heart which has become divided not only in theory but also in fact.

The case for open records and open adoption builds on this. In adoption, as in any sphere of human life, biology may not be destiny, but it cannot be denied except at the expense of a *real* loss. To in any way cut off or deprive any human person of this *nature* or dimension of their being is an attack on their personhood. Such a person will not only grieve the loss of this *nature,* they will also grieve and feel accurately that they have lost not only a dimension of themselves but their personhood as well. Philosophically, this explains why many adoptees not only feel a sense of loss or diminution as a result of their adoptive status, but feel as well that their *being,* that is, the core of who they are, is somehow damaged. Further, with this idea, we can understand why even open adoption, open records, and search and reunions do not completely *heal* this loss. Reconnection to one's *biology,* that is one's history and heritage, does not automatically equate with reintegration and ultimately transcendence of the body-soul, nature-spirit split in one's own unique, irreplaceable personhood.

Without the doctrine of the person, adoption remains entrapped in the fruitless and emotionally divisive nature-nurture controversy. Which is more important? Which contributes more to our identity? The answer is neither. Our identity proceeds from our personhood in which both are constitutively present.

When Bartholet attacks *biologism,* what really fuels her animus, is the sense of *entitlement* to which biology sometimes gives rise. There is some reality to this, as in the truism flesh of my flesh and blood of my blood, etc. *"Blood is thicker than water"* is not completely meaningless nor was it coined by the "People against adoption front." Rather, it expresses an essential truth about the human condition. But this sense of entitlement should not be allowed to debase itself into a sense that children are the property of the biological parent. It should suggest, however, the very common sense axiom that except under extreme conditions children are better off being raised by their natural parents.

Because she conflates *entitlement* with *biologism,* Bartholet evades entirely the question of whether or not an adoption system; especially an adoption system that would always privilege whoever has *possession* of the child when birth and adoptive parent rights conflict, might also be based on the false philosophy that any child is ever the property of anyone. Concealing what is all too often a *we've got her, she's ours* attitude behind the idea of nurture and the sentiment of "we're the only parents she has ever known" does not alter the case. Anyone can be guilty of thinking of their child as property. It does not matter whether the parent is a parent by adoption or birth. Indeed, to think in this way, at some time and in some degree, is probably universal among parents and merely reflects our imperfect state. That we neither act on this belief nor build an adoption system that either overtly or covertly perpetuates and rewards it is the ultimate goal.

If I have any reason to be optimistic about adoption reform, in spite of the overwhelming counter reaction occurring today, it is because I think that in the end our humanity always surfaces, the heart overrules the head. Ms. Bartholet's humanity does surface in many parts of her book, especially, in several beautiful passages that concern her own children. But in her head, she is a social engineer with too little suspicion of social controls that are in the *child's best interest* and too much belief in their power. The heart will always find a way. It even found a way into this book. But not often. The social engineer casts a long shadow.

The Neighborhood of the Heart

Fostering and the Future of Children

T. S. Eliot once defined the task of poetry as a "raid on the inarticulate" by which I suppose he meant that poetry oracularly evokes zones of being whose nature and even existence ordinarily escape our contemplation. In this brief note, I wish to mount a similar campaign, although the range of my ambitions is far more limited than that of the poet's, whose scope is as broad and dazzling as is the sky. My concern is only with a unique but neglected groove of instinct whose influence on the relationships obtaining in our society between adults and children could conceivably be immense and renewing.

To this groove of instinct, I'd like to give the name the "instinct to foster." The instinct to foster. *The fostering instinct.* What is its nature? And what is its likeness to the more familiar instinct to reproduce and parent? Whatever it is, fostering is something generous and good. It's something luminously human.

It's what the teacher feels in her devotion to students who all too often just don't seem to give a damn; the coach experiences it too in his late night dim bulbed but undefeated exasperation with his irresponsible star athlete; the foster mother feels it as she rocks a child whose nervous sleep recalls the nightmare of addiction; the driver stuck in traffic knows it when in the midst of his grimacing frustration he grins and waves at a wide-eyed child staring whimsically out of another car; and the grocery shopper feels it too when she cringes at the slap administered one aisle over to a crying, begging child; the Big Brother expresses it and the Big Sister; so too the Scout leader, the youth minister, the police and parole officer, the social worker, the community volunteer.

Whether it be as part of our job, if we're involved with youth services, or in the form of a wistfully or indignantly felt tenderness for the stranger's child whose path unexpectedly moves across our own, all of us on some level of our being, care and care deeply, not only about our own children, whom we of course adore, but also about all children whether biologically, culturally, or racially connected to us or not. Red and yellow, black and white, on some level of the soul, precious in all our sight.

With its warmth and service the fostering instinct very much resembles the instinct to parent. But it is not identical with parenting; for although, when asked, it can sometimes keep watch for parents who because of life's unexpected installments of disappointments and of pain, momentarily cannot cope or who are unavailable or absent, more routinely fostering coexists with parenting, to whom it extends a helping hand, a kindly word, or even on occasion unwelcome, interference. Rather than substituting for parenting, fostering serves, fostering supports, and fostering supplements.

In what follows I wish to clarify and celebrate this instinct; first, by distilling from the wisdom of literature three symbols whose transcendent beauty and nobility are such that I hope they will inspire you; and, then, second, to analyze some of those factors that prevent the emergence of conscious fostering; and, finally, I aim to sound a flourish, a call to arms, about how each of us today might better foster in a way that strengthens our community.

*

Do you know the lore of fostering? Because my time is short, my list is brief and drawn from the ways of my own heart and loves. But I urge you to consult the lore yourself, the ways of your own culture and traditions and then, to water them with tears of joy and recognition and the broad, fine rivers of your own childhood reminiscences.

Do you know the beautiful tale of Saint Bridget, the foster mother of Christ? Legend has it that while a child, she could neither walk nor talk, and so, as is the way so often with those who are a little different, she was ostracized by being set adrift in a small raft upon the great Irish sea. There she drifted hungry, thirsty, until coming ashore at Iona, where she at once began not to walk and talk, as do those whose only thought is to be like others. Instead, she began to skip and sing:

> *I am but a little child*
> *Yet my mantle shall be laid*
> *Upon the Lord of the World,*
> *The King of the elements Himself*
> *And I will give Him peace.*

Raised in the grove of sacred knowledge, Bridget flourished in her lessons. But one day while following the white flash of a dove through a bosque of flowering trees, she came upon a strange and foreign desert land where she assisted at the birth of the Christ Child whose tender brow she baptized with three drops of holy water. And, then, because the cows in this desert land gave no milk, Bridget sang the "Runes of Paradise" so that the milk flowed freely. And, then, with the child wrapped securely in her arms and swaddled in her own blue blanket, Bridget fed the child from the foaming bucket with the milk ecstatic with the bliss of paradise. Thus, Bridget was called midwife to Mary, Fostermother of Christ.

Now, from Scotland south to Faulkner's mythical Mississippi to encounter old Sam Fathers, part slave, part chief, and fosterer. Here he is with young Ike, Faulkner's archetypal hero, as the boy is poised with not a little fear and trembling at the edge of manhood. Together they would sit on cold fall days beneath the tall bare trees while the close fierce stars leaned near, and Sam would talk to the boy telling him the lost history of the people.

"The boy would never question him; Sam did not react to questions. The boy would just wait and listen and Sam would begin talking about the people whom he had not had time to ever know and so could not remember.

"And as he talked. . . And as he talked about those old times and those dead and vanished men of another race from either that the boy knew, gradually to the boy those old times would cease to be old times and would become a part of the boy's present, not only as if they'd happened yesterday, but as if they were still happening, the men who talked through them actually walking in breath and air and casting actual shadow on the earth they had not quitted. And more, as if some of them had not happened, yet would occur tomorrow until at last it would seem to the boy that he himself had not come into existence yet. . ."

By stories linking today to yesterday: by stories that build a bridge into tomorrow – we foster souls of children as they struggle to subdue their fears and overcome their isolation.

And now to another place in Faulkner, to a moment of supreme tension and decision between a father and a son whose bond of love has been strained by the boy's lie and theft of a car and three day spree away from home without permission. Now in the cellar of the house, the son and father face each other, with the father with a razor strap in hand. And then a knock.

"The door was not locked, but Grandfather's father had taught him, and he had taught Father, and Father had taught me that no door required a lock: the closed door itself was sufficient until you were invited to enter it. But Grandfather didn't wait, not this time."

"No," Father said. "This is what you would have done to me twenty years ago."

"Maybe I have more sense now," Grandfather said. "Persuade Alison to go on back upstairs and stop snivelling." Then Father was gone, the door closed again. Grandfather sat in the rocking chair: not fat, but with just the right amount of paunch to fill the white waistcoat and make the heavy gold watch chain hang right.

"I lied," I said.

"Come here," he said.

"I can't," I said. "I lied, I tell you."

"I know it," he said.

"Then do something about it. Do anything, just so it's something."

"I can't," he said.

"There aint anything to do? Not anything?"

"I didn't say that," Grandfather said, "I said I couldn't. You can."

"What?" I said. "How can I forget it? Tell me how to."

"You can't," he said. "Nothing is ever forgotten. Nothing is ever lost. It's too valuable."

"Then what can I do?"

"Live with it," Grandfather said.

"Live with it? You mean, forever? For the rest of my life? Not ever to get rid of it? Never? I can't. Don't you see I can't?"

"Yes you can," he said. "You will. A gentleman always does. A gentleman can live through anything. He faces anything. A gentleman accepts the responsibility of his actions and bears the burden of their consequences, even when he did not himself instigate them but only acquiesced to them, didn't say No though he knew he should. Come here." Then I was crying hard, bawling, standing (no: kneeling; I was that tall now) between his knees, one of his hands at the small of my back, the other at the back of my head holding my face down against his stiff collar and shirt and I could smell him – the starch and shaving lotion and chewing tobacco and benzine where Grandmother or Delphine had cleaned a spot from his coat, and always a faint smell of whiskey. . . "There," he said at last. "That should have emptied the cistern. Now go wash your face. A gentleman cries too, but he always washes his face."

By relating these tales, my purpose is frankly to delight you, but while delighting you to aid us all in recovery of the knowledge that a tradition of fostering does exist. In other places and at other times, humankind has understood that while growing up we all need sometimes more than a parent can provide. And in other places and at other times, humankind has also understood that it is the duty and glory of others to provide it, as the Saint feeds the Christ Child with the milk of Paradise, as Sam Fathers feeds Ike with the stories of the people, and as Grandfather provides the discipline that leaves its mark upon the heart instead of upon the backside.

Neither Bridget nor Ike were related to the child to whom they gave such inordinate, irreplaceable gifts and while the boy's grandfather was, of course, blood kin to him, nonetheless, to discipline a child is the right and responsibility today associated only with parents. To interfere at such a moment between father and son in order to stop a whipping is not an interference on which most of us as contemporary parents would look too kindly. The right to discipline has become a right that we as parents guard most jealously.

But why? Why is help so often viewed as interference? If Bridget were to appear today and offer a strange child a glass of milk, it is not the Saint of whom we would be thinking but the Witch with her poisonous apple. Does the rule "Don't take candy from strangers," apply to saints with cups bearing milk of paradise? And to disappear into the woods with an older man of a different race in order to hear his stories, what sort of response would we make to that? And grandparents who tell us when and when not to discipline?

When did family boundaries become so fixed, so brittle? When did parents become so frightened of the world? And when did parents become so jealous of their privileges?

While some might quickly counter that it became this way only when the world went crazy, only when our society began to teem with inexhaustible unsavoriness, only when the streets grew slick with nightmare, only when the bogeyman moved in next door, so that it is only responsible today to keep your guard up while distrusting everyone. So that it's only responsible now to overprotect.

Perhaps. But perhaps this bewitchment of the world expresses a far more intractable deeper problem. But whatever the case, we must dispel it, for we are raising a generation that is learning not at their parents' knees but in front of the television set, that the world is a hostile, toxic dangerous place which leaves the young with only two alternatives: to retreat, to isolate themselves behind the walls of whatever is most familiar, of whomever is most like them in culture or in color, or they must arm themselves, not only in the literal sense, although we have too much of that, but also in the metaphorical sense of hardening their hearts and thickening their skins until they think of nothing but of survival, of success, and of power in a world that respects only power.

Perhaps one way of dispelling this enchantment is to perceive the living spirit of family as imprisoned by dead ideas or by ideas that ought to be dead and would be dead if we were more consistently aware of them.

What idea do I have in mind? What idea is vexing me?

It is the error or, rather, the outrage of thinking of children as property. With its roots in much of traditional society and law, where not only children but also women were owned as property, the idea is deep seated and far reaching in legal theory. But the law would never have been invented nor would it ever stand if it did not build on some secret disposition already darkening our heart. And, of course, although we would recoil from the conscious thought, most of us do in some way regard our children as our own, as somehow belonging to us. In law, in jokes, in our unapologetically possessive language of mine, mine, mine, each of us believes that my child is mine and don't touch it.

So just as we build fences around our property, we build walls around our kids and then explain it's only for their protection. So often as parents we try to live through our children, substituting our own desires, ambitions, wishes and hopes for the children's true souls. How often it is we as parents who forge those mind forged manacles so destructive of human desire, human love and human identity.

To express the idea through a metaphor: often we try to raise our children the way we grow a garden. First, we turn over the existing ground plowing under everything already there, and then we seed with our own wishes, plans, desires, which we then fertilize, prune, pat, water, weed and eventually harvest. What we get then is what we want, but at the cost of a child's free heart.

No, the souls of children are more like wildflowers that blaze and bloom up on a hillside, or in a shady gully or sprout up in the cracks of an alley, or climb the faceless concrete of a tenement wall where no one would have thought to look. No, the true job of a parent is not so much to garden as it is to gaze in wonder, to praise with surprise and joy, to nurture and encourage and to expose to the sun and rain and all the other elements with which we might not be so familiar but to which the flower turns. When it comes to the future, not our will but their will be done.

This gentle nurturing of sun and rain, the strength of the soil, the stability of the place: this is what the fostering instinct can provide if we do not stake a claim that transforms our children into private gardens on whose high and insurmountable, encompassing wall there hangs a sign: no trespassing allowed.

If our purpose is to overcome the evil – and it is an evil and I don't hesitate to use the word, for evil is abroad in the land (just listen for its footsteps) – the evil of living our lives and constructing our laws as if children were property, the first step must be to revision the idea of family.

We must subdue the imperialism of biology, the idolatry of the blood, of blood kinship. It is not that biology doesn't count. Of course, it does. To walk and talk with one's own kind, with those from whom one drew breath and life; to know one's past, to feel as rooted and solid as an ancient tree, these are essential ingredients of human happiness. Roots give weight, stature, continuity. We all long to be among our people. But biology is not destiny. In his autobiography, the Scottish high poet Edward Muir writes, "Our minds are possessed by three mysteries: where we came from, where we are going, and, since we are not alone, but members of a countless family, how should we live with one another." To deny any one of these three essential mysteries reduces ourselves to one dimensional men or women.

As I've written elsewhere, to reduce the idea of family to blood connection, to blood kin, is to make the family one dimensional. The idea of limiting family to blood kin is in fact a relatively recent historical innovation; in fact, we might even argue aberration; for the older, far more universal meaning of family is *household* and there could be and usually were many members of one's household to whom there was no blood tie. One's family was not those to whom one felt bonded or attached, for these are metaphors drawn from the vocabulary of objects – glue bonds and objects attach – but to whom one felt close, with whom one shared the warmth of the fire, the trust of intimacy, the satisfaction of a meal, the challenge of work, the ordeal of hard times, the security of a routine, and of course, the vibrant, vital glow of love.

In these older, more traditional meanings, the symbol of the family was the *hearth* rather than the *blood.* To share a hearth together was to belong to a family.

We need to understand family not in opposition to community nor as a bulwark against but as the most intimately and lovingly and enduringly experienced form of community. But community must be the larger, more inclusive idea and in the hierarchy of values, the taller term.

Community has become an abstract idea, too much associated with politicians and bureaucrats. Community has become abstract because the old neighborhoods have disappeared. And neighborhoods sustained fostering. It was not only that everyone in the neighborhood knew you, which is the new definition of the term, as in the "hood" that you better stay out of if you don't belong, but that the adults in the neighborhood had the authority and assumed the right and responsibility to participate in all the young people's lives. Even when I was growing up thirty years ago, the neighborhood was still alive. For hours I sat in Mr. Guzick's garage while he worked with his tools and told me about life on a battleship in World War II, and also without ever mentioning it directly but only modeling it in his dignity, his kindness and his strength, he taught me a little about what it means to feel that other people don't accept you for who you are, because you see, Mr. Guzick was a Jew in a city and a time when Jews continued to subtly and sometimes not so subtly be excluded from the mainstream. There was Mr. Bowman in his overalls and Harold who while he painted told me about his years in the Navy and Mr. Hedderman who was always out in his yard after 5 o'clock, sipping iced tea and enjoying the cool of the evening; a dozen mothers who fed me, who watched me, who sheltered and protected me and a dozen other kids. Most of us forty years or older remember the neighborhoods or the suburbs and ache for their security, grieve for their passing and occasionally, when we have time and wealth enough, try to recreate them once again.

But the neighborhoods are gone. And with them has gone the normal, sanctioned medium for the expression of fostering? We can't simply go out on the front porch, into the workshop or into the garden or out to work on the car or shoot baskets or out on the lawn in the late afternoon and find ourselves with children under foot.

Children, young men and women run their own society now, so that outside of school rare is the child who has any contact at all with adult society other than his or her own parents or the parents of their friends. No Mr. Wilsons anymore.

But if the neighborhoods are gone, what can we do, those of us who wish to continue the tradition of fostering? What we can do is to create a neighborhood of hearts. *Not of houses but of hearts.* The best and brightest chance for fostering today is by joining with other adults who share the dream, who share the vision of a world where it's safe to be a child, where children have time enough to grow, food enough to eat, love enough to flourish, space enough to play, light and opportunity enough to learn, example enough to mature, to grow, as the gospel has it, in stature and in wisdom.

Now another name for this new neighborhood of hearts is the social service system. By social service system I mean all the helping professions – child care, teaching, counselling, coaching, social work, medicine and even law and law enforcement – both in their institutional and non-institutional forms. Just how far away we are from fulfilling this ideal for children is indicated by the gulf that separates the image of a neighborhood of hearts from the reality and often heartless practices of the system.

But if in the past fostering worked primarily through the neighborhoods and if it is fair to say that in the present the social services have replaced the neighborhood as the principal means by which we might foster and nurture children; and if further fostering is universally and essentially a human impulse, one that we deny both at our own and at our children's peril, then we must also say that the only way that each of us can be true to ourselves and to our nature is by committing and contributing every way possible to the social service system so that we really do make it a neighborhood of hearts.

So the question becomes what more can you do? What price are you willing to pay? What sacrifice will you be equal to? Can you give money? Can you teach? Can you coach? Are you willing to smile and reach out to every child who seems to need it? Are you willing to stand up and speak out when you see a child lost, alone, or abused? What can you do? Where can you volunteer? Can you be a tutor, a mentor, a fosterer, a foster parent, an adoptive parent? Are you willing to give your muscle and your money and your mind, your ideas and inspiration? You see it's not only for the children, it's also for yourself. To fulfill our natures as decent human beings requires it.

But at once we confront a problem: for the social services have lost the respect of the community. If we haven't already failed, we are failing: the adoption system is in shambles, beleaguered by greed and sentimentalism; the foster care system has collapsed. It is not working. Too many of our young folk, especially urban African-American kids are lost within the foster care system with their hearts shattered, their histories forgotten, and their hopes destroyed. With both the public schools and the juvenile justice system, the story is the same. And family therapy has yet to arrive at treatment equal to the Uzzi intervention which rules the streets. The most popular youth group has become the youth gang.

If the social services are not respected by the public at large, social service professionals are not respected by the young with whom we work. How could we expect the situation to be different? After generations of being urbanized, suburbanized, professionalized and dehumanized, there is just not much left to respect about the typical social service professional or volunteer. We're not that good any more at those kinds of feats and virtues whose demonstration delights a child or inspires the respect of a young man or a young woman with the hormonal rage of adolescence coursing through his or her veins. We're not strong, we're not skilled, we're not savvy, we're not streetwise. In the world as it is, down there in the streets, in trenches and in the media where young folks live, a 40-year-old city boy can't survive and frankly neither can a country boy even if as Hank Williams, Jr. said, he "can run a trout line."

One of the first rules I learned while training as a family therapist is that respect comes before love and understanding. I think the formulator of this idea is Richard Belsen. Hats off to him. Because it's invaluably true. For a parent to effectively parent a son or daughter, he or she first has to have the child's respect, for without respect the child's affection and expression of love for the parent will often fuse unattractively with the soothing courtships and manipulations of an expert con; and, in the absence of respect for his mother or father, a teenager will never understand and accept any limitations to his behavior.

Is it possible for parents to command the respect of their children? Yes. I've seen it done even in the most unfavorable, unpromising of circumstances. And if parents can do it alone, we ought as professionals to be able to do it collectively. How does one earn respect? One way and one way only: one earns respect by showing courage.

In traditional philosophy, courage is honored as the most important virtue because the expression of all the other virtues in life often depends on courage. It's fine to be honest, good, virtuous and noble when there is no cost, but when there is a cost, it takes courage to be good. Wasn't it Andrew Jackson who said, "A man with courage forms a majority of one" which I would quickly amend to say "A man or woman or child with courage forms a majority of one." The psychologist Alfred Adler defined courage as the soul of mental health.

Although courage is conventionally embodied in images of physical valor and heroic strength, philosophy knows of many different kinds of courage. But at the same time, I don't want to minimize sheer physical courage, the kind of courage displayed today by many fosterers, very often people of color, who have put themselves in the line of fire out on the streets, and in the face of drugs and gang activity where they have made a difference.

But I also want to speak of the courage of the heart, the courage that wears one's heart upon one's sleeve, the courage that reveals one's most private fears, one's most guarded vulnerabilities and stands for them, the kind of courage that acts by first saying "I'm afraid."

I want to commend as well moral courage, which I would define as the courage to keep one's word, to remain faithful to one's vow, that if one says that he's committed to some ideal or aim remains committed to the ideal or aim. This is the sublime courage of fidelity.

And sometimes the two must be combined, so that when we go back on our word, or break a solemn vow or accept a compromise in the name of diplomacy or we go along to get along, that we admit we've failed, rather than wrapping our personal failures which are after all merely the tokens of our humanity, our very human feet of clay, in bald, blatant bureaucratic euphemisms.

A third form of courage is social courage, the courage to stand up to the system. So many children today are lost in the system. The system itself has become a more hostile, alien environment than the wilderness ever was. We must model standing up to the system. And as social service professionals, we must first stand up to our own system and speak out against racial injustice, against inequities and ineptness, against the ridiculous gap between administrative and direct service salaries and against unfair distribution of funds among those who work with children when the only justification is that's the way it's always been done. If as Thoreau said most of us live quiet lives of desperation, it's because most of us live quiet lives. The time has come to speak out and if our speaking goes unheard, then to shout.

With courage we can rebuild our system. With courage we can recreate a neighborhood in everybody's heart. With courage we can metaphorically restore the old front porch where in the afternoon shade and beneath the twinkling stars every child is welcome to just come and sit awhile and from which broad friendly habitation we can keep an eye out for everyone. Let me end then with words about courage said long ago which I fear that we have forgotten. "*. . .the same basic choice of courage or compliance continually faces us all, whether we fear the anger of constituents, friends, a board of directors or our union, whenever we stand against the flow of opinion on strongly contested issues. For without belittling the courage with which men have died, we should not forget those acts of courage with which men have lived. The courage of life is often a less dramatic spectacle than the courage of a final moment; but it is not less a magnificent mixture of triumph and tragedy. A man does what he must – in spite of personal consequences, in spite of obstacles and dangers and pressures – and that is the basis of all human morality.*" The words were John F. Kennedy's, but, the voice – it can come again from you, from me.

*

Justice for Jessica

The story is familiar. A young woman facing the birth of a child whom she fears she will be unable to parent, decides to place the child for adoption. A family physician arranges for placement of the infant with a couple from a neighboring state where, because of a dubious history marred by frequent abuse, private adoptions arranged by a third party other than a licensed agency, are illegal. From all accounts, the prospective adoptive couple seem to be decent people eager to provide the stability and love that is necessary for a child to flourish.

But something goes wrong, so that, as Ellen Goodman, the syndicated columnist, described it, the adoption does not go "simply and smoothly." The birthmother changes her mind. Some would say she has been 'brainwashed' by a radical adoption rights group call CUB (Concerned United Birthparents); while others who have personal knowledge of CUB will realize that the young woman's change of mind probably occurred in response to hearing about the adoption experience from those who have actually lived it.

Here the story changes. Unlike other birthparents who feel they have been pressured, this young woman appears to have the foundation for a legal challenge to the placement. In her grief and her guilt, and, perhaps, with some other private purpose in mind, she has named the wrong birthfather. She maintains she has not received proper counselling. She maintains her decision was hurried by an attorney representing the adoptive couple and by a hospital staff unfamiliar with the anguish and ambivalence that is often attendant upon the relinquishment of a child for adoption. She hopes a sympathetic public will look with suspicion on a couple traveling to another state in order to bypass the laws obtaining in their place of residence.

Having reconciled with the infant's true birthfather, with whom, at her own choice, she has had little contact during the pregnancy, the couple goes to court to reclaim the child whose adoption has not been finalized.

In Iowa, where the child was born, a court rules the infant must be returned. In Michigan, where the adoptive couple lives, a judge disagrees. A higher Michigan court decides the lower Michigan court does not have jurisdiction.

The original ruling stands. The child must be returned to the birthparents. They have a nursery waiting. Soon a couple from whom a child drew breath and life will hold that child again. Soon another couple who in good faith and with love accepted that child into their home will have nothing but their memories and their grief. Their nursery will be empty.

The child's name is Jessica. The birthmother is Cara Clausen; the birthfather is Dan Schmidt. The adoptive couple are Robby and Jan DeBoer.

What would be justice in this? What would be a just resolution?

The most compassionate view would be to honor both the child's attachment and connection to both families by defining the case in terms somewhat akin to a "difficult divorce," in a family with very young children, where although one parent receives custody, the other parent or parents, should either spouse remarry, are granted reasonable but regular visitation rights. To attempt to bar either family from contact, now, after Jessica has attached to the DeBoers just as she will remain forever bonded to the Schmidts, is clearly a miscarriage of justice. It is not in the best interest of the child.

What we all should learn from this tragedy is the critical importance of professional, disinterested counselling for both birth and adoptive parents and for the child. Adoption is always a lifelong process. Even if this adoption had gone "simply and smoothly," Jessica and her parents would all have to face the pain and the trauma that are a dimension of every adoption.

What we must remember is that both couples love this child; that both couples are doing what they believe to be right and in the best interest of Jessica. Reasonable and good intentioned people can disagree about the individual merits of this case, but what we can never disagree about and what we must never lose sight of is that love and mutual understanding are the only ways to resolve such complex, volatile matters that involve our most fundamental values and emotions. Blame and anger only blind us.

If a villain exists in this case, it is the system of adoption itself which for too long has concealed the truth about adoption. Adoption is **not** a happy solution to a problem. It is a tragedy out of which joy and happiness often emerge. But even this joy and happiness remains alloyed with pain, with grief, with loss, with heartache. Who could ever call the separation of a child from his mother a 'solution' to anything? A necessity, perhaps. A blessing even, though a mixed blessing. But never a solution.

Had Cara Clausen been told this; had a sincere attempt been made to persuade her to be truthful about Jessica's birthfather, for his legacy to the child in terms of history and continuity with the rest of the human race is irreplaceable; had Robby and Jan DeBoer understood from the beginning that roots are real even if they are only part of the story; had they themselves met Cara, looked into her eyes, shared her grief, and allowed her to feel the love for her child already mounting in their hearts, which would lift Jessica up into a future in which Cara, and Tom, should he desire it, would be allowed to play a significant part, sharing not in the right and responsibilities of parenting, but in a common love and connection to their child, the pages of this story may have been stained with fewer tears.

An adoption system built on sentimentality and secrecy; an adoption system that pits birth and adoptive parents against each other; an adoption system forever unable, it would seem, to acknowledge the simple human right of adoptees to have access to their own history, is the reason for the tragedy of this child and for the pain of these two families. We have no one to blame but ourselves.

Eyes That Shine

Every so often when working in adoption, one chances upon a kind of luminous detail whose effect is such as to take one deeper into the mystery of the phenomena.

For me such a time occurred not so long ago when I was present at a first meeting between an adoptive family whose child, a girl, was two years old, and the birthparents of the child. The adoption, obviously was open, and there had occurred many an exchange of pictures and letters, but a first meeting had been long delayed because of the birthfather's reluctance about which he could really never say very much except that he felt that it wasn't time. But the time had come now, prompted, I think, by the little girl's recent birthday, whose passing had raised the ghosts of all those unhappy, unhealing feelings.

So now we were gathering, me first into the room, with the adoptive family whose apprehension played itself out in the clearing of throats, the drumming of fingers, and the constant attention to the child whose curiosity was exploring and absorbing everything including what we were discovering to be the excessively delicate pages of a book on my desk.

Time ticked by. Ticked by. Ticked by. The couple was late, so late that we were only a few sighs away from beginning to feel that peculiar mix of relief and guilt and anger that comes from having successfully avoided something potentially difficult but which you really wanted to do because you know it's right.

But then the knock on the door, the energy jolt, the exchange of greetings, and in they come, shuffling, awkward, tense but friendly. And then their eyes on the little girl, and the adoptive parents' eyes as well were on the little girl who immediately climbs into her mother's lap.

The meeting goes off very well. As I sit with my back against the window so as to be at least somewhat in the shadows, I think that this is the kind of meeting whose details will be shared tomorrow in the kitchen, at staff, with other workers as a way of reassuring ourselves that yes, we are doing the right thing, that open adoption is the right thing, and that none of us needs to feel guilty or worried about this very ambiguous business of taking children from one family and placing them with another. But then it comes, the detail unexpected, the detail that won't be quite so easy to share, the detail that will leave me shaken and wanting very badly to be out of this business once and for all.

The little girl is sitting at her mother's feet, having relaxed somewhat, with her mood falling in with the warm cadences of the genuinely friendly, trusting conversation going on between her parents and the strangers whose love for her is as soft, embracing and unintrusive as the light streaming in through the windows. And then, she climbs up onto her birthfather's lap.

He is a hard man, a laborer, solid, strong, with rough, calloused hands. His wife is a very pretty woman, with a soft mouth and wide brown eyes. They are middle-aged. This is not their first or only child. They have four others, three boys and a daughter. This was a child they felt they could not keep without sending their entire family over the edge into the want and hunger and homelessness that remains a daily worry that seizes them each morning as soon as they open their eyes.

For a second, the man sits stiff, but then his strength and love welcome the little girl into his arms. And then, he begins to cry. Quietly, so quietly, that his daughter doesn't realize it for a moment, but as she does she slips out of his arms and seeks the refuge of her mother who, as she draws her up, reaches out for a second to gently touch the man who looks at her and then puts down a curtain of control and politeness. And then the meeting ends with promises to meet again – perhaps around Christmas.

Do you think you know why this man was crying? I thought I did. I thought he was crying for himself, for his wife and for his family and for their other daughter and for the loss they had all endured. I thought the man was grieving.

And in a fashion he was, though his grief was not of the kind about which I have read much in the literature.

One of the advantages of being a therapist working for a large public agency is it's a little like being a big city bus driver with a regular route; that is, you get to see a real cross section of humanity and see or hear a different story almost every day and you also have your regulars whose lives begin to weave in and out of yours. Private practice, I would think, is a little more like driving your own car: fewer stories, fewer strangers, less chance to hear years later how it all turned out. So I did get to hear later how it had all turned out. I did get to hear more about the reason why a strong and stoic man had gently cried.

It was not from him, of course. It was from his wife, who, like many wives, unfortunately, spent a lot of time explaining her husband's feelings. "You know what it was," she said to me a few days later when by phone we were talking about the meeting. "He wasn't crying for her. He was crying for our children. He'd never seen one of them so happy. They've had to deal with so much. We just can't do for them the way we want to. I think it was her eyes," the mother said. "*Her eyes. Her eyes.* My children's eyes have never shone like that. Never." And then she, too, begins to cry.

Eyes that shine. It's an image I can't get out of my mind. I think of all the children whose eyes will never shine – the unwanted ones, of course, the ones who suffer and who are hungry and homeless and subject to the kinds of abuse whose horror and degradations are almost unimaginable if you haven't seen them up close, first hand; but I'm thinking also of the children who are wanted and who are loved but whose eyes will never shine, because life is often cruel, even when parents are decent and loving. Life takes a toll; our hearts pay the bill. We can get overdrawn; and that's when children suffer. Is it wrong for such parents to give a child away, to place them into the arms and hearts of someone to whom life, for whatever reasons, has been more kind and who want to share that kindness and their love with a child?

Perhaps. Perhaps not. I just don't know. But I do know in this one case about a little girl with eyes that shine.

Conclusion

I once heard Bishop Tutu, the Anglican South African Bishop and Civil Rights Activist, define the goal of the spiritual life as the effort to make the world more hospitable to love. A better definition I have never encountered.

One final word about love itself, since it is love, I think, and our attempt to live our love that motivates adoption practice, even if that love be ill or willfully expressed and thus destructive.

All too often, with our own hearts constrained by insecurities, doubts and rancors, we think of love as if it were a quantity, an exhaustible supply with only so much to go around. And if love were indeed like that, adoptive parents would have every right and reason to fear the birthparents, because a child's love for their birthparents could not help but reduce the love that their child feels for them. It would be impossible not to feel in competition and it would be impossible not to feel that such competition would create both crises and confusion from which a child, whose nature is almost by definition to be vulnerable, ought to be protected.

But, of course, love is not like that at all. Instead love *"bears all things, believes all things, hopes all things, endures all things. Love never fails."* Instead love is like the light, a warm, radiant effulgence of which there is always and eternally enough to go around, a divine, inexhaustible, inextricable beam — unless, that is, one chooses either to block the light or to disappear into the shadows. An old mystic saying defines sin as the wall we build between ourselves and the light. All darkness is of our own making.

And so adoptive parents need not fear the birthparents, for the love that a child will feel for these mysterious strangers, whose presence in reality, no matter how erratic or infrequent it might be, confirms that roots are real while reassuring of unbroken continuity with the rest of the human race, in no way diminishes the love that the child will feel for the parents whose strength and love surrounds them in the way of a blanket on a cold winter night. Their parents' arms give them security; their parents' eyes give them hope. Their parents' dreams give them a future. And in the case of an open adoption, their parents' courage gives them a past and thus an opportunity to heal their hearts. *Love, not the law is what makes an adoptive parent real.*

No, love is like the light. So what is open adoption? Nothing more and nothing less than the attempt to live true to that eternal verity taught by every spiritual master and felt in every human heart: that children truly are the light of our lives.

*

SUGGESTED READINGS

Aigner, Hal. Adoption in America: Coming of Age. Paradigm, 1986.

Arms, Suzanne. Adoption: A Handful of Hope. Celestial Arts, 1990.

Benet, Mary K. The Politics of Adoption. Free Press, 1976.

Boswell, John. The Kindness of Strangers. Harvard University Press, 1989.

Brodzinsky David M., and Marshall D. Schecter, eds. The Psychology of Adoption. Oxford University Press, 1990.

Burgess, Linda C. Adoption: How It Works. Burgess Books, 1989.

Campbell, Lee. Understanding the Birthparent. Concerned United Birthparents (CUB), 1979.

Dunn Charles. The Foundling and The Werewolf: A Literary-Historical Study of Guillaumc de Palerne. Toronto, 1960. Univerisity of Toronto Studies and Texts.

Dusky, Lorraine. Birthmark. M. Evans, 1979.

Fisher, Florence. The Search For Anna Fisher. Harper-Row, 1988.

Goody, Jack. "Adoption in Cross-Cultural Perspective." Comparative Studies in Society and History 11, (1969).

Gritter, James. Adoption Without Fear. Corona Publishing Company, 1989.

Herlihy, David. Medieval Households. Cambridge, 1985.

Hibbs, Euthymia D. Adoption: Historical Perspectives. International University. Press, 1991.

Jafee, Benson, and David Fanshel. How They Fared in Adoption: A Follow-Up Study. Bks Demand UMI.

Kirk, H. David. Adoptive Kinship: A Modern Institution in Need of Reform. Ben-Simon, 1985.

Kirk, H. David. Shared Fate: A Theory & Method of Adoptive Relationships. Ben-Simon, 1984.

Kittson, Ruth. Orphan Voyage. Orphan Voyage, 1981.

Kittson, Ruth. They Serve Fugitively. Orphan Voyage, 1959.

Klapisch-Zuber, Christiane. Women, Family, and Ritual in Renaissance Italy. Trans. Lydia Cochrane. Chicago, 1985.

Lacey, W.K. The Family in Classical Greece. Ithaca, 1968.

Laslett, Peter, et al., eds. Bastardy and Its Comparative History. Cambridge, Mass., 1980.

Lifton, Betty Jean. Lost & Found: The Adoption Experience. Harper-Row, 1988.

Lifton, Betty Jean. Twice Born: Memoirs of an Adopted Daughter. Penguin, 1977.

Lynch, Joseph. Godparents and Kinship in Early Medieval Europe. Princeton, 1986.

McClure, Ruth. Coram's Children: The London Foundling Hospital in the Eighteenth Century. New Haven. 1981.

McLaren, Angus. Reproductive Rituals. Methuen & Co. Ltd, 1984.

Musser, Sandra K. and Smith, Norm. Heartcries From the Adoption Triangle. Jan Publication, 1986.

Musser, Sandra K. and Zimmerman, Steve. What Kind of Love is This? Jan Publication, 1982.

Orme, N. From Childhood to Chivalry: The Education of the English Kings and Aristocracy, 1066-1530. London, 1984.

Pannor, Reuben, Fred Massarik and Byron Evens. The Unmarried Father. Springer, 1978.

Paton, Jean. The Adopted Break Silence. Orphan Voyage, 1954.

Pentikainen, Juha. The Nordic Dead Child Tradition. Helsinki, 1968.

Pollock, L.A. The Forgotten Children: Parent-Child Relations from 1500-1900. Cambridge, 1983.

Redford, Donald. "The Literary Motif of the Exposed Child." Numen: International Review of the History of Religions 14 (1967).

Riben, Marsha. The Dark Side of Adoption. Harlo Press, 1988.

Rillera, Mary Jo and Sharon Kaplan. Cooperative Adoption. Triadoption Publications, 1984.

Rothman, Shiela M. and David J. The Origins of Adoption: Two Reports. Garland Publication, 1987.

Schmitt, Jean-Claude. The Holy Greyhound: Guinefort, Healer of Children Since the Thirteenth Century. Trans. Martin Thom. New York, 1983.

Shahar, Shulamith. Childhood In The Middle Ages. Routledge, 1990.

Simpson, Eileen. Orphans: Real and Imaginary. Weidenfeld & Nicolson, 1987.

Sorosky, Arthur D., et. al. The Adoption Triangle: Sealed or Opened Records: How They Affect Adoptees, Birthparents & Adoptive Parents. 2nd edition, Corona Publishing Company, 1989.

Tansey, Beve, ed. Exploring Adoptive Family Life: The Collected Adoption Papers of H. David Kirk. Ben-Simon, 1988.

Teague, Alan. Social Change, Social Work & The Adoption of Children. Gower Publishing Company, 1989.

Waltner, Ann. "The Adoption of Children in Ming and Early Ch'ing China." Ph.D. Dissertation, University of California, Berkeley, 1981.

Watts, Tim J. The Right of Adoptees to Know Their Biological Parents: A Bibliography. Vance Biblios, 1988.

ALSO AVAILABLE

Adoption: Charms and Rituals for Healing

By Randolph W. Severson

Featuring:

Fire on the Dream Cloud:
A Story about Birth Families and Loss
Heart Words: An Adoption Fable

Drawing both on poetry and scholarship, together with his experience as a family therapist working at an adoption agency, the author mixes stories and poems, and insights and images to create a poetic-philosophic overview of all the colors and contours of this most familiar but also very mysterious reality. Chapters and other luminous details feature insights and interventions relating to pain, loss, grief, the special vulnerability of the adoptive family, search, open adoption, family adoption day, adoption in the ancient world, and the healing power of stories.

In this book, psychotherapy becomes finally what is was meant to be -- the art of listening, storytelling, of deep soul reflection, feeling and love. While addressed to the millions of people touched by the gifts and problems of adoption, anyone drawn to the concerns of the human soul will find this work absolutely magical.

Robert J. Sardello, Ph.D.
Author, Stirring of Culture and Facing the World with Soul

"an encyclopedic knowledge, a profound understanding. But more than this, a peace and hope born of his own serenity and selfless regard for others."

Charles Fischer, Ph.D.
Professor of Psychology, Franciscan University

ALSO AVAILABLE

Can't You Sit Still? Adoption and Attention Deficit Hyperactivity Disorder

By Randolph W. Severson

"This remarkable booklet would be useful to the parent of any child with a learning disability, although it is specifically written for adoptive parents. Dr. Severson shows deep empathy and understanding both for the parents and for the child, whom he sees as a whole and valuable human being, not just a collection of symptoms to be managed.
.......Although this book contains many practical tips for dealing with a hyperactive child, and with schools, therapists, medication, etc., the main emphasis is on a positive inner view, on the importance of pride both to the child and the parents. The author uses a mixture of anecdotes from his own life and practice, and pertinent poetry and quotations from sources as diverse as Wordsworth, Sean O'Casey, and Isak Dinensen to bring his ideas to life. For example, King Henry II of England is described as someone who was a hyperactive child! The point is made that this type of behavior was often a benefit, not a problem, in rural or pre-industrial societies.
.........Sports are strongly recommended for the learning-disabled child, especially individual sports like martial arts, which I have found greatly benefited my own learning-disabled son. The questions of diet and medication are treated with moderation and common sense, neither dismissing nor seeing either as a panacea for learning problems.
.......The special problems of adoptive parents, and of learning-disabled adoptees, are also treated with thoroughness and understanding. The many theories for the prevalence of learning problems among adoptees are discussed, but no blame is fixed, and the continued emphasis is on what will best help the child to cope with her special circumstances. Dr. Severson continually stresses the active role of parents -- that they are the true "experts," and that they need constant vigilance in dealing with the many professional experts they will encounter.
......He ends his book with these words: 'With more heart, more courage, with more compassion, with more creativity and more common sense, we can together create a world where more children will thrive. It begins one day and one child at a time.' This booklet will help parents put those ideals into practice." AdoptNet

". . .factual, warm, helpful and full of hope."
Sharon Kaplan, Director
Parenting Resources

ALSO AVAILABLE

Then I Too Will Remember The Story of a Young Man's Death by Cancer

By Randolph W. Severson

One of the most tragic events in life is the death of a child.

This is a story about a young man's death, but also a story about the journey of his heart into a place of imagination, love, courage and healing. Further, it is a story about his family, his mother's love, his father's grief and how they come in time to accept his death and to find some meaning in it.

Shuttling back and forth between the worlds of myth, legend and ordinary reality, this is a story that will make you and your family laugh and cry, wonder and imagine, even as it renews your faith in the dignity and transcendence of the human soul.

ALSO AVAILABLE

A Mighty Time

By Randolph W. Severson

"This easy-to-read booklet is a must for every adoptive parent. Mr. Severson has a good sense about adolescents and their development stages. He presents a four point plan to help parents talk about sex with their teenager."

COCA Reports/Spring 1992